MOTHERHOOD, CHILDHOOD, AND SELFHOOD

Motherhood, Childhood, and Selfhood

Psychoanalytic Reflections

Mali Mann

International Psychoanalytic Books (IPBooks)
New York • http://www.IPBooks.net

MOTHERHOOD, CHILDHOOD, AND SELFHOOD
Psychoanalytic Reflections

Published by IPBooks, Queens, NY
Online at: www.IPBooks.net

Typesetting by Noel S. Morado

ISBN: 978-1-969031-56-4

To
Andrea Parisa
My beloved, Creative, Wise, Kind,
& Humanitarian Daughter

Contents

Acknowledgments

My colleague Dr. Salman Akhtar motivated me to put my published papers together in a book. I had the honor of contributing book chapters to his numerous contributions to psychoanalytic literature. Salman's encouragement during the pandemic and my grieving process of losing my beloved husband, Dr. William Stover, who struggled for five years with Lewy Body Dementia, was a significant source of strength and empowerment.

I sincerely thank Salman, who has been an inspiring figure in my psychoanalytic life.

I am deeply grateful to my patients for their trust and resilience, to my daughter for her unwavering support, and to my personal friends for their comforting presence during a difficult time.

About the Author

Mali Mann is a psychiatrist and psychoanalyst, who specializes in adult, adolescent, and child psychoanalysis. Her role as a training and supervising psychoanalyst and child supervisor at the San Francisco Center for Psychoanalysis is just one aspect of her international influence. Her practice, based in Los Altos, California, is a hub for psychodynamic psychotherapy and psychoanalysis for children, adolescents, and adults. Her international recognition as a chair of the inter-Committee on Child Abuse/Neglect and her supervisory roles in adult and child psychoanalysis, along with her contributions to the field through faculty supervision at the Western Regional Child Psychoanalytic organization, Tehran Institute of Psychoanalysis, and her teaching position at the China America Psychoanalytic Alliance, underscore her global impact. Mali's professional interests lie in the application of psychoanalysis.

As a clinical faculty and adjunct clinical professor at Stanford University School of Medicine, Department of Psychiatry and Behavioral Science, Mali Mann plays a pivotal role in shaping the next generation of mental-health professionals. Her responsibilities include supervising and teaching medical ethics to psychiatry residents and child psychiatry fellows, a testament to her unwavering commitment to ethical practice and her academic prowess.

She has published several chapters and psychoanalytic papers, such as "Immigrant parents and their emigrant adolescents: The tension of inner and outer worlds" (2004); "Shame veiled and unveiled" (2010), "Aggression in children: Origins, manifestation, and management through play" (2011), and "The formation and development of individual and ethnic identity: Insights from psychiatry and psychoanalytic theory" (2006). Her award-winning edited book, *Psychoanalytic Aspects of Assisted Reproductive Technology* was published in 2014 and she has published two poetry books: *Whisper, Forget Me Not* and *A Path with No Name*, a collection of her poems and paintings. Her poems have also been published in several journals, including the book *Walking with the Shadows, Leaving Them Behind*, for which she was selected by the Pegasus Physician Writers at Stanford University. Her latest book, *My Pony, Keran*, is a semi-autobiographical children's book.

She has been a member of the Flying Doctors (Los Medicos Voladores) for nearly three decades. She and her late husband, Dr. William James Stover, traveled to orphanages in impoverished South America and Mexico to offer medical help to children and their families.

In her spare time, Mali Mann indulges in artistic pursuits, painting abstract expressionism, figurative art, and encaustic monograms. Her art, which has been exhibited in US galleries and won several awards, is a testament to her diverse tale nts and serves as an inspiration to others.

Introduction

This book is structured into three essential parts, each delving into the psychoanalytic understanding of motherhood, childhood, and selfhood. These parts are crucial in understanding the complex dynamics at play in modern family formations.

In today's modern era, psychoanalysts play a pivotal role in defining and understanding the complexities of new motherhood and the innovative ways of forming a family. Their expertise and insights are invaluable in navigating the challenges of modern family dynamics. The term "motherhood" covers a diverse range of meanings. Some women are having children later in life and are encountering infertility. The pollution in our environment, food, and air contributes to this infertility, leading to increased stress and pressure in individuals' lives. This stress can also affect fertility. Infertility has reached an epidemic proportion, and statistically, there are one in five couples in northern America who are infertile, and 20 percent of all marriages are facing infertility. Reproductive technology has revolutionized family formation, allowing individuals to build families despite infertility. This technological advancement has redefined traditional family-making and opened new avenues for parenthood, reshaping the modern family structure. Infertile couples now get involved in assisted reproductive technology to achieve parenthood.

Immigrant mothers experience another form of motherhood. The impact of immigration on their mothering is a complex experience driven by an interaction of intra-psychic, interpersonal, and sociocultural factors. The literature shows that in the context of immigration the experience of marginal or traumatic stress among immigrant women has a significant impact on the lives of many immigrant mothers and their offspring. It is important to note that mothers transmit cultural values, traditions, belief systems, and modes of behavior. Therefore, there is a need to understand the nuances of the experience of immigrant mothering and the role they play in their children's identity formation. It is necessary to consider aspects of the maternal experience shared across cultural contexts. There is a vast difference between traditional views on motherhood and parenting and those in modern times.

Some mothers go through the challenges of handling motherhood single-handedly. There needs to be sufficient attention given to the women's inner sense of autonomy from a psychoanalytic perspective, looking at the woman's independence, and its attribution to a sense of self. This often overlaps with the understanding of identity, separation–individuation, attachment patterns, and object relations, which are all essential aspects of development. In addition, there is the contribution of gender identity and sexual orientation, and the rapidly changing landscape of gay marriages and lesbian motherhood that has resulted in social and legal changes. One aspect of this is family formation via surrogate parenting. Surrogacy is a contentious issue and is outlawed in several European countries, including Italy, Spain, France, and Germany.

It is vital to attend to the foundations of the self-laid down by a robust attachment to the primary caregiver, which involves our continuous memories in the hearts of our loved ones. Also essential is the significant role played by fathers in family dynamics, which should be included in all future literature. Those fathers with the capability of maternal identification with nurturing aspects of their personalities can also contribute to consolidating their daughters' separation-individuations as mothers do. Recognizing and valuing their role is crucial for fostering a sense of respect and understanding.

Part II on childhood highlights issues related to child abuse, shame, and aggression. A mobilization of national concern and resources began in 1975 in the US to alleviate child abuse. The problem of child abuse has its roots in ancient history but it did not receive widespread public recognition in the US until 1962 when a description of "Battered Child Syndrome" entered the media. Violence inflicted on children was finally viewed as a public health problem that affected family members, parents, and children. The Child Abuse Prevention Act was signed into law, the National Center on Child Abuse and Neglect came into operation, and the National Committee for Prevention of Child Abuse was established. For the first time, the federal government made long-term grants of millions of dollars available to programs designed to prevent child abuse, identify cases, and alleviate the consequences to the families of abused children by effective intervention. Many states launched public education campaigns to encourage the reporting of suspected cases of abuse and the detection of early signs.

These changes have been important but so much more remains to be done in all aspects of this universal problem. At times, it feels as though barely a dent has been made in dealing with the problem of child abuse, especially with regard to abusive parents. Primary prevention programs to keep abuse and neglect from happening remain few and in some areas of the world, they are non-existent.

On the topic of shame, I have described cases of children who demonstrate its important developmental aspects. Shame can be traced from the birth of human existence and its cultural origins. In our clinical work, it's crucial to recognize and address potential collusion with patients' sense of shame. This awareness of the tendency to collude in ignoring shame is a key tool for therapists in dealing with this crucial affect, ensuring we are fully informed and aware in our practice. Shame, as an affect, is a deeply searing and painful experience that is intricately linked with an individual's self-awareness.

Children and adults who undergo repeated shame experiences are more likely to have a substitute affect, such as rage or depression, to disavow their feelings of shame. As clinicians, we need to be more observant of shame experiences in children. We recognize how difficult it can be for adult patients to access feelings of shame and the memories that go with them. We need to make an active effort to open the feelings of shame to further analytic exploration with both adults and children. Shame, often seen as a negative emotion, can also be a powerful and positive motivator for human interaction and engagement, sparking curiosity and intrigue in its potential. There is a significant need for further clinical research to understand this complex phenomenon and I hope these chapters will inspire future investigation into this critical study area.

Children who are subjected to the experience of repeated shame defensively turn to the affect of aggression. This is one of many causes that can lead to aggression in children, who are not emotionally equipped to manage their rageful feelings.

Part III looks at selfhood with a particular focus on ethnic identity formation and the role of an immigrant mother in her adolescent child's identity formation. Immigration, being a complex biopsychosocial process, can mobilize the destabilization of psychic structure and profoundly influence identity formation. This destabilization is a gradual process that requires resiliency to restructure the ego and establish an optimal psychic equilibrium. Immigrant mothers carry the shadow of their former lives within their newly found identity in the host country. The nature of a mother's past life in her homeland, combined with the slow but steady change in identity as an immigrant, creates a complexity of experience that involves learning a language later in life and other cultural variants. These influences, in turn, can affect their children's separation-individuation and adolescent passage processes in the new country.

This book is crucial in raising awareness and understanding of the complex issues surrounding motherhood, childhood, and children's identity formation. It piques the interest of psychoanalysts, stimulates their analytical thinking, and furthers their education in psychoanalytic training, challenging them to give these issues the attention they deserve. It also aims to raise awareness among all those who work with children and parents, ensuring they are conscious and informed about these important developmental issues.

The book includes several clinical cases that represent children's development, especially children who come from immigrant families and present specific problems in response to their mothers' unmetabolized loss of their mother lands and their incomplete mourning. The frequency of traumatic experiences is not consistently recognized, and analytical clinicians would benefit by reviewing the complexity of human development, particularly young children and their mothers. We psychoanalysts want to offer the best treatment action to our patients who need psychoanalytic exploration. And this "best treatment action" involves a comprehensive understanding of the patient's history, a supportive therapeutic environment, and a focus on the patient's unconscious conflicts and early experiences.

There is an opportunity to learn about the early developmental process, which expands and improves our work with children and adolescents and increases our enjoyment of analyzing them.

Donald Winnicott, whose extensive writings on child analysis are very well appreciated globally, showed us how he found the opportunity to obtain psychoanalytic knowledge from working with and paying close attention to children's play and how he was able to help children. I enjoy learning about his work and consider him as my guiding light. This work builds on his foundations and shows how by engaging closely with children and adolescents, we can find much more to learn.

PART I

MOTHERHOOD

CHAPTER 1

Modern motherhood[1]

Today, psychoanalysis faces new challenges in how to define modern motherhood, parenthood, and family formation. We see a new perspective on motherhood and the evolving roles of mothers. Psychoanalytic theories about mothers can be modified to understand the challenges of new motherhood for today's mothers. Some mothers partake in their mother roles as single mothers. And there are adopting mothers, foster mothers, surrogate mothers, immigrant mothers, lesbian mothers, and women who become mothers with the help of a donor egg.

Our new world creates an acceptance for a variety of people to procreate. People with genetic problems, same-gender couples, donor eggs, donor sperm, embryo donors, and surrogates who carry the fetus are all involved in a particular form of procreation. They participate in the making of a new family that is different from traditional family-making patterns. This new form of extended family complex raises questions about our psychoanalytic understandings of the pre-oedipal mother, the oedipal complex, and attachment patterns to primary caregivers.

---

1 Originally published as Mann, M. (2016). Modern motherhood, modern mothering, and new family constellations: A concluding commentary. In: S. Akhtar (Ed.) *The New Motherhoods: Patterns of Early Child Care in Contemporary Culture* (pp. 187–200). London: Rowman & Littlefield. Copyright © 2016 by Rowman & Littlefield. All rights reserved.

People involved in assisted reproductive technology possibly claim a share of parenthood and entitlement to the child. This new phenomenon affects the parents' and siblings' dynamics, as well as the overall larger family matrix. Does it mean the new family structure needs reconfiguration? What are the culturally acceptable ways of relating to each family member, and how do various roles get negotiated?

The child coming out of this new family structure is also in need of help to identify the primary caregiver, to feel safe and ideally form a secure attachment. What is communicated to the child about his or her origin, and what is kept secret for reasons related to parental, unresolved psychological conflicts, also potentially impact their developmental trajectory.

These different family dynamics are rather new and their members enter into uncharted territory. They cannot rely on inherited historical generational wisdom or experience. The parents conceivably have to rely more on the expertise of mental-health professionals for guidance, since the older generation of grandparents are at a loss, not knowing how to negotiate their roles in such newly made and newly defined families. From the earlier psychoanalysts, Freud's, Melanie Klein's, and Anna Freud's work was focused on oedipal conflict and constellation. However, it is worth mentioning the contemporary developmental analyst Diane Ehrensaft's work. In her book of 2008, *Mommies, Daddies, Donors, Surrogates: Answering Tough Questions and Building Strong Families,* (2008b), she criticizes the orthodox psychoanalytic concept of the oedipal stage and alerts clinicians to expand its scope to include the importance of psychological theories of psychosocial and psychosexual development to accommodate to the realities of modern-day families. We have to face the new reality of today's modern phenomena and be willing to accept the increase of non-traditional families. Additionally, we need to think about how our ideas about developmental perspectives—such as some aspects of Margaret Mahler's separation-individuation process and its formulation—might need to be modified or adjusted. separation-individuation theory views the intra-psychic experience from an interpersonal perspective and conversely can consider interpersonal elements from an intra-psychic point of view. Furthermore, it provides a conceptual frame that can accommodate diverse perspectives, from dyadic, pre-oedipal to triadic, oedipal modes of relatedness.

I will review the following distinguished contributors who offer their divergent conceptual perspectives in contemporary psychoanalytic thought about parenthood, motherhood, and modern family structure.

Henri Parens, in "The changing morphology of parenthood: Its implications for separation-individuation theory" (2015), contributed his rich, detailed and persuasive exposition of his view on the psychodynamics of the child's earliest postnatal attachments, both in earlier eras and today, and his recognition of the changing morphology of parenthood and re-consideration of central aspects of Mahler's separation-individuation theory. He expresses his viewpoint and suggests possible changes in defining parenthood, childrearing, and childcare-giving in today's modern times. In his research in the 1970s, following advances in the women's movement, he proposed that each family must decide for itself how to divide and distribute parenting labors, since now both mother and father work outside the home. While childbearing and breastfeeding will always be the role of the mother, the part that has changed pertains to those twin parenting functions, *childrearing* and *caregiving*. Of these twin functions, Parens addresses *caregiving*. Caregiving is the foremost critical factor in what becomes the child's mental health and emotional life. While emotional investment in the child is perceived by the child in average, expectable childrearing, it is especially in caregiving that the child perceives the parent's investment of meaning and emotional value in them. The parent does this by being especially attuned and contingently responsive to the child's experiences of both good and bad. But in the end, parenting requires reflective thinking about how to help the child cope with stress, learn self-control, adapt, and ideally be prepared to mentalize. Another factor that also enters the equation is parents' expectations, which concern their determination to achieve their parenting goals.

The 1980s are known for significant scholarly contributions to the understanding of the effect of direct and ongoing paternal involvement on child development. James Herzog, Kyle D. Pruett, and Mereille Abelin contributed to Mahler's symposiums with an emphasis on the role of the father. The primacy of the mother has undoubtedly been the focus in the past decades, but there has been an important shift in the early relationship between infants and their fathers.

Parens's (2015) reflections on separation-individuation first made him review the wide scope of the neuroscience of all species as having been prewired toward infant attachment, which led him to the "adaptive plasticity" previously theorized by René Spitz. In 1945, Spitz published a landmark article in which he suggested that babies cared for in institutions commonly miss adaptive plasticity. Spitz's observational research findings had an important impact on our understanding of the structuring of libidinal objects. He believed the infant's brain-based instinctive mechanism elicits the social smile. He also elaborated on his twin anxiety reactions, namely separation anxiety and stranger anxiety. Parens's careful review of Spitz's research demonstrates that he respects an eminent researcher whose work deserves proper recognition.

Parens also raises an important and provocative question regarding a possible revision of Mahler's separation-individuation theory. "Toward some revision of separation-individuation theory," he critiques Mahler's theory regarding the early phases of development. While a direct reference to a specific publication titled "Toward some revision of separation-individuation theory" is challenging to find through a general search, multiple sources corroborate the nature of Parens's critique of Mahler's work regarding the normal autistic and symbiotic phases of development, as discussed on ResearchGate. He argues that infant observation research doesn't support the idea of a completely autistic state in the earliest phase, but rather suggests that infants show early interest in objects, as noted in the ResearchGate article. He also points out that Mahler's concept of the symbiotic phase didn't adequately address the reciprocal gratification that mother and infant derive from their interaction, according to ResearchGate.

"Parens reviews Mahler's two phases that have been challenged both from within ego psychology and by attachment theorists. He challenges what Mahler called the "normal autistic phase." In his infant observation research, he notes that infants react to the object with interest, which refutes an autistic state. He suggested to Mahler that the term "primary narcissistic stage," reflective of the activity of the infant's healthy primary narcissism, could better describe what she intended to describe. However, no other investigator has changed the term. Parens also asserts that Mahler's application of the term "symbiotic phase" did not intend to address the fact that the mother was reciprocally deriving gratification from having a baby, or from her co-existence with it. He proposes that "symbiosis" or, as he prefers to call it, "the subjective experience" of "being one with the object," may be experienced with multiple objects in that initial process, and that these objects bring with them "libidinal object constancy" that provides lifelong "inner sustainment" (Parens, 1977). Parens emphasizes that early-life-engaged fathers, adoptive mothers and fathers, and parents of variable gender dispositions can all bring "a sense of oneness with the object" into the life of the child. He therefore suggests widening the concept of the "symbiosis" of separation-individuation beyond the primacy of only the mother.

Here, I would like to switch to another important form of motherhood: immigrant mothers and the impact of immigration on their mothering. Pratyusha Tummala-Narra and Milena Claudius describe immigrant motherhood as a complex experience driven by an interaction of intra-psychic, interpersonal, and sociocultural factors. Tummala-Narra and Claudius's psychoanalytic perspective that integrates contextual understandings is critical to addressing the intra-psychic and interpersonal lives of both mothers who immigrate to the US and women who become mothers' post-migration. They review the literature concerning the context of immigration, including the experience of marginality and traumatic stress among immigrant women that has a significant impact on the lives of many immigrant mothers. They explore the internal life of mothers and the complicated ways in which immigrant mothers negotiate the mothering process and their identities in the face of cultural change and upheaval.

About 51 percent of the foreign-born population in the US are women, contributing to a global trend of a "feminization of migration" (International Organization for Migration, 2006). While female migration to the United States has been consistently and independently of men, in order to meet economic demands rather than to join partners or family (American Psychological Association, 2012; International Organization for Migration, 2006; Sam, 2006).

The layered contexts and circumstances surrounding decisions to migrate to another country shape women's intra-psychic experiences of mothering. However, the psychic life of immigrant mothers in the contemporary US is typically invisible to the public eye as a unique set of contextual stressors can impinge on the mothering process. While mothering can be an intense and sometimes overwhelming experience for women from any sociocultural background, mothering in an immigrant context contains additional layers of complexity. First-generation immigrant mothers face language and communication barriers, and both first- and second-generation immigrant mothers can face social isolation as they traverse multiple conflicting cultural systems regarding parenting (Tsai, Chen, & Huang, 2011; Tummala-Narra, 2004). The acculturation process for immigrant (first-generation) and immigrant-origin (second-generation) mothers is determined by the influence of multiple contexts, such as home; neighborhood; physical and psychological distance from country of origin; access to support networks; and work environments (Akhtar, 2011). While the multiple contexts within the ecology of immigrant mothers in the US influence each other, a profound sense of isolation can develop due to marked environmental and cultural changes that affect mothers and their families (Levi, 2014; Marks et al., 2014).

Tummala-Narra and Claudius elaborate on the issues of gender and power within the family among immigrant women who migrate from countries of origin with less gender egalitarianism, relative to that in the US, in order to access an increased sense of choice and freedom in education and employment, increased sexual freedom, and new ways of defining the self (American Psychological Association, 2012; Tummala-Narra, 2013).

While migration can provide tremendous opportunity for women's growth, greater autonomy, and gender equivalence, immigrant women have also been subject to systems of oppression, including racism and sexism (Tummala-Narra, 2013). Many women face traumatic experiences at varying points in the migration process (pre-migration, in transit to the new country, and post-migration) (Perez-Foster, 2001). Women's experiences of physical and sexual violence have been identified as a public health crisis on a global scale. Immigrant women have been subjected to trauma and marginality even though the host country provided them opportunities to grow, and to acquire gender equivalence and autonomy. Many immigrant women and girls endure silence and isolation concerning violence within their homes; ethnic and/or religious communities; and broader, mainstream society. Challenges with language and communication, lack of knowledge regarding, or access to, resources and services, and cultural beliefs concerning violence against women can all serve as barriers to seeking and receiving support (American Psychological Association, 2012; Tummala-Narra, 2011). For mothers who have a history of being traumatized emotionally, physically, or sexually, the experience of raising children in a new country can intensify internal affective experiences and relational experiences with the child (e.g., attunement and responding to the child), all of which can be overwhelmed by concerns for the children's safety, complicating the children's negotiations for autonomy and independence. In particular, many immigrant mothers struggle with parenting in isolation, away from extended family support, and with intensified anxiety about both losing their children and losing a sense of parental authority (Ackman, 2012; Levi, 2014).

There is a need to understand the nuances of the experience of immigrant mothering. It is necessary to consider aspects of the maternal experience that are shared across cultural contexts. Although traditional views on motherhood and parenting more broadly have been challenged, and fathers generally have become more involved in childcare in many regions of the world, mothering continues to be associated with the conception of women as primary caretakers (Confortini & Ruane 2014, Ruddick 1995). It is important to note that mothers are often transmitters of cultural values, traditions, beliefs, and modes of behavior, even in cases where fathers are highly involved with parenting. As such, for many women, mothering is a critical part of their identities (Tummala-Narra, 2004, 2009). Exploring the internal, affective world of mothers as shaped by contextual realities lies at the core of understanding the reactions and behaviors of mothers. Several scholars have written about the essential need that mothers have toward protecting their children from harm. Janna Smith (2003) has underscored the ways in which mothers' emotional lives, on both conscious and unconscious levels, center on the physical survival of their infants and children. Daniel Stern (2005) has further noted the importance of older, more experienced mothers for women who are new to motherhood, particularly as they help new mothers bear fear and anxiety about the infant's survival. While early theories dismissed these embedded fears for the child's survival as neurotic, pathological, or emblematic of the mother's narcissism, contemporary psychoanalytic theorists have highlighted the fact that the mother's preoccupation with the child's safety, and her vigilance in safeguarding her child, is an essential organizing principle of motherhood that promotes the child's development. Stern (2005) describes the "motherhood constellation" as one that is analogous to falling in love. He suggests that "most mothers either fall in love with their babies, or want to, or wish they could, or regret that they have not" (Stern, 2005, p. 4). By likening the mother's psychic experience to falling in love, Stern emphasizes the intersubjective quality of the mother–infant relationship, which is composed of mutually created and understood language and symbolism.

The formation of maternal identity in the immigrant context also encompasses conflicts between dominant parenting styles in the culture of origin and those in the new cultural environment. Over the past several decades, there has been an increasing emphasis in the US on an intensive style of mothering in which a central task of motherhood is to develop the ability to emotionally attune to the needs of the child and to fulfill his or her physical and psychological needs. In modern times, there are women who want to be independent mothers, often characterized as those who choose motherhood—biologically or through adoption—and work to build a career with little or no support from their community. Tummala-Narra, 2009). D. W. Winnicott's (1971) concepts of "good-enough" mothering and primary maternal preoccupation support the primacy of the mother–infant/mother–child emotional relationship. The quality of affective experience is therefore at the heart of psychoanalytic models of optimal mothering. Yet these conceptions have often excluded the effects of external realities, especially stress associated with loss of and separation from loved ones; trauma; and cultural upheaval. There are many examples of mothers who are not able to mourn the loss of their motherlands. Access to the mental-health system is a big challenge to go through a thorough mourning process to enable themselves to live a happy life.

The immigrant mother's experience is complex and is influenced by an interaction of intra-psychic, interpersonal, and sociocultural factors. Psychoanalytic perspectives offer an important lens into the internal life of immigrant mothers, and how the subjectivity of the mother interacts with that of the child. In the immigrant context, layers of hope, connection, marginalization, isolation, and anxiety shape these subjectivities. It is important that the psychoanalyst recognizes the importance of the migration process (pre-, transitioning, and post-), the losses and separations incurred in this process, and the interwoven nature of intra-psychic, interpersonal, and cultural conflicts.

Mary Kay O'Neil, in her paper "Single mothers and women's autonomy," mentions that single motherhood is not a new phenomenon but a socially accepted kind of mothering. Her comment about single mothers, or, as she refers to these women, "sole support mothers," is based on an outcome study of fifty-nine women in the US who participated in a program (called Project Chance) that provided safe, secure, affordable housing and supportive activities for their children while the mothers engaged in post-secondary education. Having given birth, these women chose to raise their children on their own. Certainly, single motherhood poses difficult financial and psychosocial challenges for both mother and child. The results for many include dependence on the welfare system, poverty and social pathology that can extend for generations.

As we all know, and as underlined by UNICEF:

The lives of women are inextricably linked to the well-being of children. If they are not educated, if they are not healthy, if they are not empowered, the children are the ones who suffer. (UNICEF 2006):

Previously, not only was there general societal disapproval but also within psychoanalysis there was a rather judgmental anthologizing attitude toward single motherhood.

(Amado, et al., 2022, pp, 4–5) quotes Leontine Young (1954), who noted that women today mainly do not become pregnant out of wedlock through ignorance or irresponsibility. Some of them do, but in the great majority of cases the action is purposeful, often subconsciously, and has its origin in the woman's family background. The unmarried mother *wants* a baby, specifically an out-of-wedlock baby, *without* a husband. The psychoanalytic conception of "normality" has now changed, especially in the light of *in-vitro* fertilization and same-sex parenting. Given the profound societal and psychoanalytic changes in attitudes toward sexual behavior, toward women bearing and raising their children on their own, as well as marked changes in methods and circumstances around pregnancy, women are more able to make conscious, ego-syntonic, mature decisions about wanting to have a baby and raising a child on their own.

Within psychoanalysis, sufficient attention has not been given to women's inner sense of autonomy until more recent years. Freud had much difficulty understanding a woman's development separate from that of a man. In recent times, there have been opportunities to focus on the complex developmental process by which girls develop into independent, autonomous women. Autonomy, one attribute of the self, includes the partially overlapping concepts of a sense of identity, separation-individuation, narcissism, attachment, and object relations. O'Neal, from her clinical experience and her sample of "sole support mothers," is able to identify at least six contributors to this complex process. These contributors are named motherhood, adaptive defenses, maternal attachment, resilience, opportunity, support, and reciprocal relationships. O'Neil stresses the importance of becoming a mother as a major contributor to the development of a woman's autonomous self. She emphasizes the importance of adaptive defenses, resilience, opportunity, and the right kind of support, and lastly the capacity for reciprocal relationship. She highlights the importance of a recognition that dependency is not necessarily incompatible with autonomy, and nor is independence equivalent to autonomy. True autonomy has to do with an inner sense of wholeness, a woman's capacity to grow in self-confidence as a person, whether or not she is in a relationship or desirable circumstances. Autonomy is both intra-psychic and intersubjective, which includes reciprocal relationships and the capacity to love and be loved. True autonomy is not achieved without the capacity for reciprocal attachment, and this capacity is not dependent on current wished-for relationships. The optimal sense of autonomy gives one the coping ability to work through the inevitable sadness after an unpredictable loss.

There have been more recent psychoanalytic writers who have emphasized the importance of maternal attachment in girls' internalization process of maternal objects. One example of such a writer is Nancy Chodorow, who contributes a sophisticated review of gender identity, sexual orientation, and motherhood in her paper "Modern families: Reflection on gender identity, sexual orientation and motherhood." She muses on the idea of lesbian motherhood as a phenomenon specific to modern families. Her contribution is persuasive, and she agrees with numerous authors who have written on this topic that in today's time we are experiencing a "Gayby Boom." The rapidly changing landscape of gay marriage and lesbian motherhood has resulted in social change at such a rapid pace that LGBT family law changes quite frequently. The psychoanalytic discussion of women raising babies together dates back as far as 1945 when Helene Deutsch wrote her two volumes of *The Psychology of Women*. She brought to the attention of the psychoanalytic culture of her time that some women decide to raise adopted children without having to resort to male inclusion. The intentional use of reproductive technology has replaced the shame of an early twentieth-century out-of-wedlock pregnancy.

Deborah Glazer, in her paper, relates that motherhood can have different meanings for different women. Some women have a powerful desire for pregnancy, which may or may not coincide with the desire to nurture a child. Some women, as implied earlier, can have a desire to mother but no desire to conceive, carry, or nurse. Glazer presents several interesting case vignettes to demonstrate how the developmental backgrounds of her cases influenced their decision about motherhood and parenting. Additionally, their intra-psychic issues are directly relevant to the ideas about motherhood. Glazer notes that we have moved away from the idea that pathological development causes homosexuality, but that it continues to be important to explore the ways that the recognition of same-sex desire in today's cultural context can have a negative effect on the experience of the self and the development of intimate relationships. To parent or not parent remains to be a crucial question among lesbian couples. Once they decide to have a baby, they must explore how to achieve the goal. They must negotiate if they want to be biologically related to the child and how they can go about finding a known or unknown donor. Different women find different aspects of motherhood important and there are powerful implications both intra-psychically and for a lesbian relationship. Once the baby arrives, the lesbian couple, like other couples, must navigate the move from dyad to triad.

Glazer's other cases are presented to show how modern families navigate gender roles in the context of family dynamics. Modern families do not always mirror the traditional heterosexual family. The children of these modern families come in contact with other families and become aware that their family is different from those of their classmates and friends. However, like traditional families, modern families also have to contend with divorce and custody. In such situations, the maternal roles could become exchangeable in the face of the family restructuring aim.

Glazer believes that, in our current social climate, there are special developmental stressors faced by girls who grow up to be lesbian. These issues can affect self-esteem, self-regard, and gender experience in ways that can influence the formation of loving relationships, along with creating families and raising children. Glazer also believes that there is a need to bear in mind that the patients we treat today are presenting inner worlds that were developed in their childhoods, in times that were more openly hostile toward homosexuality, and not in the current state of the rapidly changing social environment as it relates to increased LGBT rights and privileges.

As we know, the recent and rapid advances in reproductive technologies confront us with the need to understand their complex psychological impact on motherhood, on children who are born through these procedures, and on families. In the first chapter of my book *Psychoanalytic Aspects of Assisted Reproductive Technology* (Mann, 2014), called "Psychoanalytic understanding of repeated in-vitro fertilization trials, failures, and repetition compulsion," I discussed how some women resort to repeated in-vitro fertilization trials in order to achieve motherhood. As a physician and psychoanalyst, I became aware of some of my women patients' trouble accepting that, despite their strong desire to become mothers, they were infertile. After a drawn-out attempt to have their own children, they resort to assisted reproductive technology, surrogacy, and as a last resort the adoption process. Acceptance of the failure to conceive is more of a challenge for some patients than others, although often there may never be a final acceptance.

In today's modern time, there are many methods to achieve motherhood and become a parent. In the last two decades, making use of scientifically refined modern methods of assisted reproductive technology has increased chances of success, increasing the numbers of positive outcomes. However, studies have shown that, during treatment, infertility is experienced as an emotional and social burden. Little research has been conducted into the long-term psychological consequences of such treatments. There is much room for research into the long-term consequences of these interventions on the inner lives of women who want to experience motherhood. Having to enter and deal with the medical system is undoubtedly stressful, and conceivably is experienced as a traumatic life event. In some infertile cases, women who dreamed of becoming mothers face the lost years and the large financial costs involved in trying to achieve pregnancy. Some try to re-envision their lives in the light of their involuntary childlessness, and to consider life scenarios other than biological parenthood. Infertility can turn into a monthly assault on feelings of femininity and can provoke a sense of identity crisis. Women who fail to conceive may question their value as women, seeing themselves as "defective."

Some infertile individuals whose infertility is related to their advanced age use alternative procedures such as in-vitro fertilization (IVF). Approximately one in fifty births in Sweden, one in sixty births in Australia, and one in eighty to a hundred births in the US now result from IVF. In 2003, more than 100,000 IVF cycles were reported from 399 clinics in the US, resulting in the births of more than 48,000 babies. IVF is now the treatment that leads to the highest pregnancy rate per cycle (Van Voorhis, 2007). Egg donation was introduced in the 1980s, increasing the possibility of pregnancy and childbearing for many women. Many of the women receiving these donations were older and had delayed childbearing for reasons such as establishing careers, personal conflict, and ambivalent feelings about becoming mothers. The use of surrogates—women who carry a pregnancy for another individual or couple—generates further possibilities for women unable to conceive. In today's world, many women want to establish themselves in their careers and choose to postpone reproductive goals until later. When they then face reproductive failure, they become extremely anxious, especially when the biological clock is ticking away faster and faster. The narcissistic injury is deep and debases their self-representation and their body image. Women are affected profoundly by fertility failure. They carry with them the identification linkage with their primary pre-oedipal maternal object, wanting to become a parent. Clinically, we see girls who play mother roles in fantasy. Once a woman's pregnancy wishes are frustrated, the denial of an infertile self-image could potentially lead to crisis. The way in which these women react to the trauma of their infertility will determine several factors, including how they choose to use a donor egg, donor sperm, or surrogate mother. The character of their traumatic experience also influences the process of deciding whether they will donate their egg, their sperm, or their womb. Though the reasoning varies among theories, experts agree that the ability to become a mother is essential to believing that one is viable as a woman. Freud (1938) made passing reference to the subject of human reproduction and pregnancy. The primacy of sexuality in human life for Freud is reflected in his belief that the wish for a child in the woman represents the symbolic substitution for the missing penis, a wish for reparation and completion. Deutsch (1945) questioned this reparative function of the woman's procreative life.

She made it clear that the woman's urge to become pregnant and bear a child represents the essentially feminine quality of receptiveness, a biophysiological concept, the bedrock of femininity. Benedek (1952) and Bibring et al. (1961), pioneers in the study of women's reproductive drive, saw pregnancy as a developmental crisis, and subsequent writers such as Notman and Lester (1988, pp. 357–366) seem to accept this view.

In severely traumatized women, the wish to be pregnant is not necessarily connected to the wish for a child, as seen by Pines (1982). Pregnancy, instead, is simply seen as an effort to repair the narcissistic injury of early life. Pines elaborated on the mother–daughter relationship as the locus of psychic conflict in women who abort habitually. Pre-oedipal dynamics were discussed and identified by Lester and Notman (1986) as causing anxieties during the early stages of pregnancy. In her paper "Infertility in the age of technology" (1999), Zallusky highlighted the effect of infertility on the analytic process. She elaborates on the permeability of the boundaries between analyst and patient, and between fantasy and action, in psychoanalytic work with women who are infertile and resort to assisted reproductive technology. The immense stress of infertility can trigger regressions to earlier stages of psychological development. Intense feelings of envy and shame conflict with their roots in childhood, bringing about a disturbance to the person's sense of self-identity. As Freud stated, the ego "is first and foremost a body ego" (1923b, p. 27).

Ehrensaft (2008a) described the feelings and fantasies of parents in relation to having another, outside party involved in conception. She described a stirring up of fantasies of a *ménage à trois*. She observed that the egg donation or the surrogate could stir up fantasies of the other. Thinking of the sperm as sperm may be defensive against thinking of the sperm as coming from another whole person. Those who succeed in becoming mothers would have to develop an effective way to cope with their past failed attempts at getting pregnant. The mother, children and family members have to process, metabolize, and think through the shared reality of their constructed new family matrix. The continuous reprocessing of new ways of dealing with the modern family construct can promote healthier cognitive and emotional development.

There is a crucial need for new ways of thinking as women enter into a new era of motherhood. The definition of "motherhood" has become widened. We need to think in a complex and multidimensional way about this uniquely personal experience with new psychosocial and perhaps political implications.

Conclusion

In this chapter, I have reviewed the work of several contributors: Parens, who raised an evocative and important question regarding a possible revision of Mahler's separation-individuation theory and its central impact on mother–infant dyadic experience; Tummala-Narra and Claudius on the importance of considering the complex experience of immigrant mothers, driven by an interaction of intra-psychic, interpersonal and sociocultural factors; O'Neal's single mothers and women's autonomy; Glazer's modern families; and my own view of the pivotal role of the mother as a crucial figure in the pre-oedipal and early developmental vicissitudes, culminating in the establishment of object constancy.

A famous Jewish proverb says, "God could not be everywhere, so he created mothers." Mothers, mother surrogates, nannies, lesbian mothers, gay couples, and today's modern families all play an essential role in the intra-psychic lives of infants and children. In the past, mothers shared motherhood with extended family members, and for those who could afford them nannies were also part of the family circle. In the present time, as women take on responsibility outside of the home, other childcare givers have become a vital part of the modern-day family. These mother-like figures have a ubiquitous presence yet are behind the scenes and often invisible. In my work with women and mothers of modern families, I found, in the analysis of screen memories, the defensive screening of their primary caregiver's losses. After much reconstruction of these memories, one can often discern that the loss was traumatic and catastrophic. However, a review of the developmental literature pertaining to the biological mother's relationship with her infant or child reveals that the influence of other types of mother figures on biological mothers and infants are totally ignored and omitted.

Immigrant mothers' love, and their motivation to bear their losses and separation from their cultural heritage for the sake of their children's well-being in a new land, is a sign of their resilience. It also adds layers of complexities when the pursuit of financial security forces some of them to become childcare workers for those non-immigrant mothers who work.

I have left out the important role that the father plays. Ideally, they too should be included in all our future discussions. Fathers who have healthy maternal identification with nurturing aspects of their own sense of father-self are also able to contribute to the consolidation of their female offspring's separation-individuation as mothers.

CHAPTER 2

In-vitro fertilization and its psychoanalytic and psychosocial ramifications[2]

Recent advances in reproductive technology and the increased use of techniques based upon it have created a need for psychoanalytic thinking and understanding of the psychological implications of *in-vitro* fertilization (IVF) and other similar procedures. The recent and rapid advances in medical technologies confront us with the mandate to understand their complex impact on women and their children.

As a physician and psychoanalyst, I became aware of my patients' trouble accepting their infertility after drawn-out, continued attempts to have children. The acceptance of failure in conceiving is more of a challenge for some patients than others, although there can never be a final acceptance. The denial of their failure as a couple to conceive can become a long process, with unfinished mourning throughout their life cycle.

The two cases in this chapter in particular illustrate how infertility traumata are re-experienced. Unconscious self-induced

---

2 Originally published as Mann, M. (2014). Psychoanalytic understanding of repeated in-vitro fertilization trials, failures, and repetition compulsion. In: M. Mann (Ed.) *Psychoanalytic Aspects of Assisted Reproductive Technology* (pp. 3–18). Abingdon, UK: Routledge. Copyright © 2014 by Routledge. Reproduced by permission of Taylor & Francis Group.

traumatization resulted from the compulsion to repeat an earlier repressed trauma.

Freud inferred the existence of motivation beyond the pleasure principle. In 1920, he postulated that "the principle of *Repetition Compulsion* in the unconscious mind, based upon instinctual activity and probably inherent in the very nature of the instincts [is] a principle powerful enough to overrule the pleasure-principle." Building on his 1914 article "Recollecting, repeating and working through," Freud highlighted how the "patient cannot remember the whole of what is repressed in him, and is obliged to *repeat* the repressed material as a contemporary experience instead of ... *remembering* it as something belonging to the past: a compulsion to repeat."

Those individuals who can better accept their infertility without significant psychological complications often resort to other methods of becoming parents to fulfill their lifelong expectation. Some may take an alternative step and adopt someone else's child. Some infertile individuals whose infertility is related to their advanced age use alternative procedures such as IVF. In today's world, many women want to establish themselves in their careers and choose to postpone reproductive goals until later. When they face reproductive failure, they become extremely anxious, especially when the biological clock is ticking away faster and faster. The narcissistic injury is deep and debases their belief system about self-representation and their body image. Women are affected profoundly by infertility failure. They carry with them the identification linkage with their primary pre-oedipal maternal object, wanting to become a parent. We see clinically girls who play mother roles in fantasy. Once a woman's pregnancy wishes are frustrated, the denial of an infertile self-image can lead to crisis.

The way in which these women react to the trauma of their infertility will determine a number of factors, including how they choose to use a donor egg, donor sperm, or surrogate mother. The character of their traumatic experience also depends upon the process of deciding who will donate their egg, their sperm, or their womb.

Though the reasoning varies among theories, and although others disagree, many experts suggest that the ability to become a mother is essential to believing that one is viable as a woman. Freud (1938) made passing reference to the subject of human reproduction and pregnancy. The primacy of sexuality in human life for Freud is reflected in his belief that the wish for a child in the woman represents the symbolic substitution for the missing penis—a wish for reparation and completion. Helene Deutsch (1945) questioned this reparative function of women's procreative life, however. She made it clear that the woman's urge to become pregnant and bear a child represents the essentially feminine quality of receptiveness, a biophysiological concept, the bedrock of femininity. Meanwhile, Benedek (1952) and Bibring et al. (1961), pioneers in the study of women's reproductive drive, saw pregnancy as a developmental crisis, and subsequent writers seem to accept this view (Notman & Lester, 1988).

In severely traumatized women, the wish to be pregnant is not necessarily connected to the wish for a child, as seen by Pines (1982). Pregnancy, instead, is simply seen as an effort to repair the narcissistic injury of early life. Pines (1982) elaborated on the mother–daughter relationship as the locus of psychic conflict in women who abort habitually. Pre-oedipal dynamics were discussed and identified by Eva Lester and Malkah Notman as causing anxieties during the early stages of pregnancy (Lester & Notman, 1986; Notman & Lester, 1988).

In her paper "Infertility in the age of technology" (1999), Sharon Zallusky highlighted the effect of infertility on the analytic process. She elaborates on the permeability of the boundaries between analyst and patient and between fantasy and action in psychoanalytic work with women who are infertile and resort to "assisted reproductive technology" (ART).

The immense stress of infertility can trigger regressions to earlier stages of psychological development. Intense feelings of envy and shame conflict with their roots in childhood, bringing about a disturbance to the person's sense of self-identity. As Freud stated, the ego "is first and foremost a body ego" (1923b, p. 27). The earliest way in which we know ourselves is through our body.

In a 2009 panel on "Current perspectives on infertility," in which the motivations for childbearing were discussed in relation to ART, Jane Kite emphasized the importance of keeping the emotional reality of the patient in view.

The entry of a third person—the doctor—into the sexual relationship, as if into the primal scene, is another theme in some of the literature. Also, in the context of surrogate mothers and/or sperm donation, Diane Ehrensaft (2008a) described the feelings and fantasies of parents in relation to having another, outside party involved in conception. She described a stirring up of fantasies of a *ménage à trois*. She observed that the egg donation or the surrogate could stir up fantasies of the other. Thinking of the sperm as just sperm may be defensive against thinking of the sperm as coming from another whole person. Ehrensaft also pointed out the importance of telling children about their origins.

Coming to terms with infertility can manifest as a problem not only for women but for both partners, and whichever partner is infertile.

In-vitro fertilization

"*In-vitro* fertilization" means "fertilization under glass" — that is, in a test tube. IVF is a technique for removing eggs from a woman, fertilizing them outside her body, and placing the fertilized egg, or embryo, directly into the uterus. All IVF procedures have four steps: ovarian stimulation, egg retrieval, fertilization, and embryo transfer.

Overcoming infertility was unimaginable just a generation or two ago. Since then, scientists have devised a way to remove the sperm and eggs and combine them. Eggs are fertilized, then frozen for future use; sperm strength can be boosted; and even women who lack ovaries may find themselves pregnant. These procedures arouse much curiosity within both the general public and the broad community of infertility and mental-health experts.

The first "test-tube baby" was born in 1978. Louise Brown was the first child to be conceived by *in-vitro* fertilization and was delivered after a full-term pregnancy. In the years since, IVF has become an important element in the vocabulary of infertility. It has become the cutting edge of modern reproductive treatment and research.

In-vitro fertilization requires intact fecundity — normal production of ova. A proportion of women in their mid-to-late thirties and early forties, in spite of their intense desire to conceive, remain infertile. Fecundity is intact in many of these women, though, and advances in reproductive technology make it possible to overcome infertility in some cases. New ground continues to be broken as research continues.

Regardless of the cause of infertility, the treatment that leads to the highest pregnancy rate per cycle is *in-vitro* fertilization. Since its inception in 1978 (Diedrich et al., 2007), there has been a remarkable increase in the number of IVF cycles worldwide. Approximately one in fifty births in Sweden, one in sixty births in Australia, and one in 80–100 births in the US now result from IVF. In 2003, more than 100,000 IVF cycles were reported from 399 clinics in the US, resulting in the birth of more than 48,000 babies. IVF is now the treatment that leads to the highest pregnancy rate per cycle (Van Voorhis, 2007). Egg donation was introduced a few years later, in the 1980s, further increasing the possibility of pregnancy and childbearing for many women. Many of the women receiving these donations were older and had delayed childbearing for reasons such as establishing careers, personal conflict, and ambivalent feelings about becoming mothers. These women, and those who had illnesses the treatment of which affected their fertility, were then able to have children. Still, egg donation brought up a great deal of controversy. In addition to ethical dilemmas, egg donation presents issues such as parental identity confusion and a compromised sense of social group belonging. I have encountered many clinical examples of this, but expounding upon them is beyond the scope of this chapter.

The use of surrogates—women who carry a pregnancy for another individual or couple—generates still further possibilities for women unable to conceive. The baby can have the genetic identity of the couple—that is, the ovum can be obtained from the woman in the couple and be fertilized by the man's sperm and then implanted in the woman who has agreed to be the surrogate—or the surrogate can supply the ovum and the sperm can be the husband's or come from a donor. This has made having a genetically related baby possible for gay couples, as well as for women who for some reason, such as repeated pregnancy loss, cannot carry a baby to term but have viable ova. It is also possible to freeze sperm, eggs, or embryos for later use.

Implanting more than one embryo increases the likelihood of having a viable pregnancy. It also increases the likelihood of multiple births, which carries greater risk. The decision to reduce one or more embryos in lieu of multiple implantations is a difficult one.

In this chapter, I do not focus on the traumatic effect of infertility. Instead, I discuss the use of multiple IVF trials despite repeated failures. One of the cases I discuss, for example, presents a serious narcissistic injury and disappointment at the discovery of infertility, which in turn affected the decision and the process of ART. A delay in decision-making created medical risks during this woman's pregnancies. She insisted on going through a second pregnancy using her own uterus to carry a fetus that came from the union of her husband's sperm and an egg from a donor, her niece.

Unexplained infertility

No matter how sophisticated the technique used to combat infertility, there are cases in which a woman remains infertile. Some causes of infertility remain beyond our understanding, even in these days of high-tech reproductive procedures. These as-yet unsolved mysteries are very frustrating to those trying to understand why some people can conceive while they cannot.

Unexplained infertility is a "diagnosis of exclusion." This means that all other known diagnoses must be eliminated before the infertility can fairly be called "unexplained." Making claims about the causality of infertility and the concept of psychogenic infertility is therefore not a useful argument for us as psychoanalysts. Conscious and unconscious hostility toward a defective male sibling (Allison, 1997), and a woman's unconscious repudiated femininity or motherhood, can be important dynamics. However, there are couples who are able to conceive naturally in spite of similar dynamics. We need to be careful not to confuse the correlational data with causality.

In recent years, infertility treatment has undergone a genuine revolution, which has raised the possibilities for empirical treatment. Today's infertility treatment is referred to as "assisted reproductive technology" (ART) and represents the joining of a hormonal therapy with a form of artificial insemination. ART is most commonly represented by intra-uterine insemination, IVF, and IVF variations.

Case 1: Jean

Jean, a married forty-eight-year-old woman, came to see me for analysis after a hiatus in her psychotherapy. During her previous years of treatment with me, when she was in her early forties, she saw me twice a week. She worked in a demanding professional field and did not know why she could not conceive. She decided to wait and try natural methods to get pregnant. She made many attempts over a long period of time to conceive without any success.

Jean's professional life was a trying and challenging one and kept her very occupied to the point that she lost track of the passing years. She did take pride in her work and wanted to appear to her colleagues as "perfect" and "flawless."

Jean's inability to conceive was very difficult for her to accept, since she thought nothing was physically wrong with her. Male factors for infertility were ruled out. It meant to her that she was defective. Jean's husband, who was in a similar professional field, was very supportive of her, and he was willing to adopt or even be childless if Jean chose not to have any children.

Jean was shame-ridden about being defective and not able to have children as her mother did. She felt intense envy toward her mother and especially her sister who was five years her senior and had one son. Her envy of pregnant women was very intense, making her angry when she encountered them.

Jean came from a deprived background both emotionally and financially. She had memories of not having food and going hungry to school. She was not sure if she was conceived out of wedlock. She believed her sister was so conceived, and in her fantasy she thought her father never married her mother.

Jean's brother was born when she was eight years old. She remembers her parents were overjoyed because they finally had a son after so many years. Jean devalued her mother for her emotional detachment but would also show guilty feelings for her rage toward her mother.

In her day-to-day interactions, Jean lacked emotional responsiveness. She tried hard to be friendly with her colleagues, as long as they praised her at work. She had many superficial friendships but she could not go beyond the surface level in relationships.

At the beginning of our work, this patient had immediate realistic concerns about dying before she could fulfill her dream of becoming a mother. Her resistance to becoming fully involved in the transference was expressed in the form of overvaluing her job, which dealt with life and death issues, in contrast to her analysis which was "just talking," a process in which "not much important action was happening."

Jean related that no matter how much insight she would gain through our work, she still needed to take action by hurrying to have children from her own eggs before it was too late. She wanted her gynecologist to give her strong fertility medication like Lupron. She went through multiple IVF procedures during this period. Each time they harvested her eggs, she would come in and boast about how many of *her own* eggs they were able to harvest. She turned a blind eye to the comments that several experts made to her about her age factor, which made her eggs unsuitable for IVF. She knew that the probability of getting a viable embryo out of her ova was very low. She vehemently defended her decision and said "I just do not want to borrow another woman's eggs."

"Borrowing" another woman's eggs would mean that Jean was inferior to that egg donor. However, after her husband suggested that perhaps they could consider an anonymous donor, she assented. Yet she waffled. If she could only find an anonymous donor from another country, perhaps she would follow through. In the end, Jean turned away from making the decision.

At this stage of our work, she was obsessed with going through many cycles of IVF without showing much interest in exploring the meaning of her desperate actions. Only after many failures in conceiving did Jean begin to wonder why she could not get pregnant. She thought she was either being punished or she was just flawed. Her almost total absence of fantasy material toward me gradually gave way to being intensely curious about my personal life after she inadvertently learned that I had a daughter. Having found out through a friend who attended a fundraising event where I was participating with my daughter, Jean imagined that I must be an attentive mother, not like her own mother who was aloof and detached. She would use technical terms to show me that she was psychologically minded and a well-read, intellectual woman. However, she would mispronounce or misuse words and quickly apologize to me for not having used the word accurately.

Jean would come to her sessions punctually, and she would get anxious when I took a break for a holiday or professional travel. She worried that I would never come back and that some disaster would separate us forever.

Gradually, the intense fear of her rage and somatic complaints gave way to uncovering the meaning of her dread over anything emotionally valuable in her life. She had intense envy of me as her analyst, and in fantasy wanted to exchange her barren existence for my rich and fulfilling life as a mother.

In one of our sessions, after complaining that she had spent so many years of her life in analysis without much change in her grief over being flawed (she still believed she was flawed), she agreed with my comment that I, too, must have failed her, having not given her the wisdom of my knowledge and experience. Like her mother, I too have given birth to a barren (analytic) child who was infertile. She acknowledged that although she agreed with much of what I said, she still had not given up on going through yet another IVF trial at her age. She was sure I could not be happy with her inability to conceive and that I would interpret it as if we both had failed.

Jean's conflict around unconscious envy of me emerged as an expression of hatred and distrust of her mother. Her sense of competitiveness also emerged as she wished to have a sense of triumph, instead of missed opportunities. Her denial of reality regarding her advanced age for a successful IVF outcome continued to take center stage in our analytic work.

Jean continued to seek the creation of a baby from her own eggs fertilized by her husband's sperm. After seven trials without any success, she regretted putting herself through such vigorous procedures for a woman her age. She became more interested in the meaning of her loss. Finally, she had to face it and go through the grief stage. She realized that she could no longer hold on to her dream—that she could neither have a genetically related child nor accept another woman's egg. After all, she could not picture herself as a nurturing mother, and she concluded that it may be for the best not to become a mother. She could not be like her own fertile mother and had to accept the reality of growing old. Finally, she was able to face her ambivalence. Jean could learn to be more nurturing to the vulnerable part of herself.

At this point, the memory of her brother's birth came up and her rivalry with him became a central theme in our work. The following is an example of how Jean characterized her envy:

Patient: I have all these mean thoughts, and I feel really bad.
Analyst: Holding onto negative thoughts makes you feel guilty.
P: It is very, very harmful to be occupied with them.
A: In our last hour you mentioned how hard it was to deal with jealousy at your brother's birth.
P: Yes, Mom was mad at me for being jealous of my brother. I am never good enough. Other people have talents and value—not me. There is this other part of me that is irrational and unkind.

There was always a feeling about my chance of getting pregnant with IVF. How many attempts I made to give birth was like pushing a pickle through a straw. How many mean thoughts I would have! I am trying to make sense of these feelings. I am flawed, but I want to be saintly and have power to make these women lose their babies or relinquish them when they are born. I have those mean, evil thoughts. I am torn again all the time.

It ran through my mind that if I had special power the technology would have worked for me. I would have gotten pregnant by now. Technology is amazing and works for others, but not me. There is a zinger in that. I did not want to have a flawed child, so maybe it was for the best that I did not get pregnant.

After many years of attempts, Jean was in a place to make a decision to adopt a one-year-old girl from China. This was a reasonable compromise for her after so many years of struggling with her desire to have her own biological child. Our analytical work had helped her to work through her early mother–daughter and oedipal conflicts.

Case 2: Fran

Fran was a forty-eight-year-old lawyer who came to see me because of depressive symptoms and a lack of romantic interest on behalf of her husband. She was hurt and angry because her husband had become emotionally involved with a woman at his work. She thought her husband had become detached because she was putting all of her effort into using reproductive technology to get pregnant.

Before her current marriage, she had been briefly married to a man who was very critical of her weight, even though she was a woman of average weight. They divorced after one year.

She remarried at forty after four years of a long-distance relationship with the man who became her husband. Her husband is an architect whom she met while she attended law school. Their sexual attraction and their individual interests in sexual activity diminished over time until they became non-existent.

Fran was interested in having children and tried without success to get pregnant in the earlier years of her marriage. She and her husband went through a reproductive/fertility workup and did intra-uterine insemination without success. In the same year, it was discovered that her uterus had three large myoma. She underwent a myomectomy and then tried to get pregnant naturally. After many months without success, she went through six IVF procedures. Each time, Fran repeated the cycle of over-stimulation of the ovaries, harvesting the eggs, *in-vitro* fertilization, and freezing of the viable embryos. She would become very hopeful, and when the transfer failed she would come to her sessions and cry in silence, going through another cycle of unfinished grief work. She would then quickly bounce back and want to try IVF again. Her denial about the loss of her youth, wanting to remain a young, fertile woman forever, was unshakable, and a sense of omnipotence governed her fantasy.

Fran came from a family of eight children. Her father was a professor and her mother was a nurse. After the first three children became school-age, her mother decided to have a second set of five children. Fran is the eldest of the second set.

Fran's father was overcritical and was frequently away traveling. Her mother was nurturing to the younger children, but the older ones were neglected. Fran had to take care of her younger siblings and did not have much private time for herself. She grew angrier each time her mother got pregnant.

Her mother's fertility was the topic of Fran's conversations with her friends and in her therapy. Fran's conflict about motherhood was significant during the early years of her marriage. There were psychological as well as physical factors in her infertility that interfered with her becoming pregnant. She dis-identified with her mother who was "fruitful, and multiplied."

As time progressed, Fran became aware of its passing, and questioned her childlessness. She became anxious and rushed to remedy her infertility by choosing to become a mother despite her inability to conceive naturally. Fran was influenced by unconscious psychological factors. Her unconscious repudiation of her femininity played an important role in her difficulty conceiving.

During her psychoanalytic treatment, Fran's developmental achievement of greater autonomy helped her to own her femininity more fully. This enabled her to see herself more as a mature woman who needed to embark on the motherhood phase of her life despite her advanced years.

Fran and her husband tried to get pregnant for over ten years. She was almost fifty when she went through her first IVF. Her doctor said the chance of success was very slim, but she wanted to go through with it anyway. When it failed, she became depressed and had to deal with the loss of a dream to have a child with her own egg. She was struggling with her own sense of omnipotence—with issues of creating life—in an ambivalent way, destroying life via denial of the reality of her advanced age. Through our analytic work, she gradually became aware of her intense repetition compulsion, accepting the reality of her aging ova and ushering her body into the menopause phase of life.

With reluctance, Fran considered going through a search for an egg donor. She decided to ask her niece to become her donor. Her niece was a young woman in her early twenties. Her niece agreed to go through the procedure for Fran with Fran's husband's sperm.

The IVF was successful and the healthy fetus was implanted in Fran's uterus. The clinic kept three more embryos for possible future pregnancies. Fran's pregnancy was normal and her delivery uneventful.

When her baby girl was born, Fran brought her to show me in my office. The girl had only a faint resemblance to her mother and Fran admitted that she looked like her niece more than her. She was thankful that her daughter was physically healthy.

This case shows a happy ending in certain respects, and yet there are many unanswered questions about Fran's family dynamics. What will happen when the child asks where she came from? When the little girl became a school-aged child, Fran was not ready to disclose the reality of her origin. She is working in treatment to understand the underlying meaning of her decision to keep it secret despite the fact that the rest of her family knows the child's origins.

Discussion

The two cases I described have a few psychological factors in common. Both women started late in their reproductive years to get pregnant. Their denials of their advanced age factor motivated both women to resort to repeated IVF trials without success. Both women had trouble accepting their infertility and insisted on having their own biological children.

Jean felt deficient and deprived. She felt it was her right to have a baby. She was envious of her mother, sister, and sister-in-law's abilities to have their own children, and she wondered why not her.

Jean was told her eggs may be defective, and her doctor advised her to use an egg donor. She was in despair and felt envious of her mother who did not have to go through a fertility workup. Jean attributed her difficulty conceiving to her mother's belief that she could not carry a baby because of her delicate body frame. After all, her mother's prophesy must have come true. At last, Jean faced her infertility while she was going through her analytical work with me.

With Fran, once her pregnancy wishes were frustrated, the denial of her infertile self-image pushed her to a potential crisis level. Her repetition compulsion is related to her unconscious envy of her mother who was "fruitful, and multiplied," having eight children, unlike her. After multiple trials, Fran accepted that the only way she could become pregnant was through a donor egg. She has not fully thought through the pros and cons of selecting a family member as her egg donor.

Both patients' narcissistic injuries were deep, and this debased their belief systems about their self-representations and their body images. They carry with them the identificatory linkage with their primary pre-oedipal maternal object, wanting to become parents. As we see clinically, girls play mother roles in fantasy. In reality, if their wishes are unfulfilled, the desire to get a different result than the one they face reaches a critical level. These conflicts propel them to try repeatedly to master the traumatic impact of their infertility.

Both cases suffered from the trauma of having to go through reproductive technology. Jean took an alternative step and adopted a child, while Fran got pregnant with a donor egg.

There are many references to repetition compulsion in psychoanalytic and psychiatric literature. I will list a selection that outlines the origin of the concept of compulsion to repeat and where it belongs in the psychic structure. Freud introduced the concept in

"Remembering, repeating and working-through" (1914g) and *Beyond the Pleasure Principle* (1920g). These texts marked a major turning point in Freud's theoretical approach. Previously, he had attributed most human behavior to the sexual instinct (the libido). In these texts, he went "beyond" the simple pleasure principle, developing his theory of drives with the addition of the death drive (referred to as "Thanatos"). He examined the relationship between repetition compulsion and the pleasure principle. Although compulsive behaviors evidently satisfied some sort of drive, they were a source of direct un-pleasure. Somehow, "no lesson has been learnt from the old experience of these activities having led only to un-pleasure. In spite of that, they are repeated, under pressure of a compulsion." Freud concluded that the human psyche includes a compulsion to repeat that is independent of the pleasure principle.

In my clinical experiences working with a small group of women who have tried using IVF multiple times without any success, I saw clear evidence that unconsciously they resort to repeating a self-induced traumatic event. A compulsion to repeat was evident in my analytical work with women who went through multiple IVFs without a successful outcome.

One of the important factors in Jean's case—repeating the use of the IVF procedure—illustrated an attempt to repair her early childhood neglect and abandonment. What is particular in Jean's case is her nonchalant attitude about the doctor's repeated warnings against using her aged eggs. Her denial was persistent, yet through our work she could finally face the reality of her infertility.

Jean's fertility process required her to be away from her analysis for a prolonged period. Though on one level this was a matter of time, on another it was psychological: the reason she needed to be away was as a defense against intimacy with her analyst. One might think of her transference as a particular form of unconscious communication, as appears in the projective identification process. She was abandoning me to fulfill her very important procreative goal of leaving her pre-oedipal mother.

Fran's case showed her significant conflict throughout her marriage. Aside from the physical factors that prolonged her attempts to get pregnant, she also had unconsciously dis-identified with her mother for fear of repeating her mother's fruitfulness in procreation.

Freud's repetition compulsion concept applies to these two cases in which the clinical phenomenon manifests with repetitive quality. However, analysis helped these two patients immensely with their aggressive conflicts, as well as with the uncovering of their past traumata.

Freud cited four empirical observations as the basis for his theories and speculations: first, dreams occur in the traumatic neuroses in which patients repeat a traumatic situation. Second, there is a tendency on the patient's part to repeat painful experiences from the past during their analyses. Third, the fate neuroses were an important notion (first theorized by Helena Deutsch as "a form of suffering imposed on the ego apparently by the outer world with a recurrent regularity [whereby] the real motive of this fate lies, as we have seen, in a constant, insoluble, inner conflict" (1965, p. 27). And fourth, certain types of children's play (such as peekaboo) support the concept of repetition compulsion.

In Burness Moore and Bernard Fine's *Psychoanalytic Terms and Concepts* (1990), the meaning of the term "repetition compulsion" was extended to include drives for mastery as well as other adaptational and maturational processes. In Freud's speculations in *Beyond the Pleasure Principle* (1920g), the repetition compulsion is presented as an explanatory concept, inextricably tied to the death instinct.

It functions as a regulatory principle, primitive in its origin and mechanisms, biologically based, and capable of overriding the pleasure/un-pleasure principle. Lawrence Kubie (1939) stated that analysts after Freud have offered such diverse interpretations of the concept "as to render it almost meaningless" (p. 390). Some contemporary authors believe that Freud's early concept of repetition compulsion is non-dynamic, negativistic and fatalistic (Inderbitzin & Levy, 1998).

Lawrence Inderbitzin and Steven Levy (1998) believe that one has to pay close attention to a more meaningful dynamic formulation that includes a consideration of the intense frustration and ensuing aggression that trauma generates, and the opportunities for aggression provided by "re-experiencing trauma." Trauma appears to take on an instinct-like role that really belongs to the aggression created by the trauma. The re-experiences of trauma contain hidden aggressive aims and gratifications (often based on identification with the aggressor), including punishment of perpetrators by inducing guilt, demand for reparation, expression of entitlement, exploitation of others, magical "control" of helplessness, and purposeful self-defeat (self-directed aggression).

A woman's failure to conceive may be related to the traumatic and unsatisfactory relationship with her mother. The re-experience of trauma by repeated use of ART such as IVF contains masked aggression, which is turned against self or others. The aggression may take the form of a demand for reparation and a magical solution to her age-induced infertility. Two clinical illustrations show how infertility traumata were re-experienced as a new version of an earlier trauma with self-induced traumatization through a compulsion to repeat.

CHAPTER 3

Egg donors and sperm donors: Parental identity formation[3]

Infertility is a medical condition that affects many aspects of human life. It affects one's relationship with the self and consequently will impact one's self-identity as a mother or father.

Individuals who resort to "assisted reproductive technology" (ART) methods will experience emotional impacts and physical, social and economic hardship in their families.

How an individual deals with these unexpected emotions depends on their personality style, coping mechanisms, and external and familial support systems.

Often, facing infertility and having to deal with its traumatic impact leads to denial and projection. The traumatic loss of one's ideal self makes it a challenge for the individual who must deal with infertility. One cannot depend solely on secondary-process thinking, as unconscious desires will always influence the decision-making process, including the choice of an egg or sperm donor.

In considering the psychological implications of ART, I will first discuss the various reproductive technologies available to couples.

---

3 Originally published as Mann, M. & Mann, A. (2014) Egg donors and sperm donors: Parental identity formation. In: M. Mann (Ed.) *Psychoanalytic Aspects of Assisted Reproductive Technology* (pp. 63–76). Abingdon, UK: Routledge. Copyright © 2014 by Routledge. Reproduced by permission of Taylor & Francis Group.

There are many resources that patients can access to learn about infertility, reproductive facts, and ART. They can also access mental-health professionals to help them with their unresolved emotions regarding their infertility and the use of an egg or sperm donor or surrogate mother.

In the United States, the American Society of Reproductive Medicine (ASRM) has been instrumental in providing specific educational resources to guide people who are facing infertility. The American Fertility Association (AFA) is an organization created to educate the public about reproductive disease and support families during struggles with infertility and adoption.

In the United Kingdom, since 2005, the child who is the product of egg donation can now find out non-identifying information about their donor at sixteen, and more detailed information, including name and address, when they reach eighteen. Although the numbers of egg donors didn't collapse after this, as feared, fewer new donors registered and there has been a shortage as demand has increased—around 1,300 women every year in the UK are treated with donated eggs—with waiting lists of around a year at some clinics, which has resulted in many women and couples seeking treatment abroad. In the UK, the number of women treated using donor eggs has hovered at around 1,300 every year since 2007 (The Guardian, 2012).

The new trend is toward openness and transparency when individuals resort to egg and sperm donors, much like adoption nowadays. More parents plan to tell such children how they were conceived. There are counseling centers that help couples with how best to do this. Anonymity and secrecy are no longer in fashion. There are still some parents who do not dare to break the secrecy, due to struggles with stigmatization, fears of forming weaker attachment bonds, and inner conflicts.

Many gay and lesbian couples pioneered openness about using donors, and many form a relationship with their child's biological parent.

Today, one in every 100 babies in the US is created through some form of *in-vitro* fertilization (IVF), and even many heterosexual couples like to tell their children this modern-day version of the facts of life (Ludden, 2011).

When and how to tell a child about biological genes depends on the child's developmental and cognitive capacity to understand the meaning of the information they receive. Dishonesty affects the child's sense of trust toward their parents. It potentially creates disequilibrium in their psychic function and object relation.

Egg donors

For women with premature ovulation failure woman's ovaries, lower ovarian reserve, or an autoimmune disease, or of advanced age, or who have been unsuccessful with IVF, or who have concerns about a genetically transmitted disease, donor-egg IVF can be considered. When *in-vitro* fertilization treatments are not effective, donor eggs can allow an infertile woman to carry a pregnancy to term and give birth. In men with deformed or absent sperm, the use of a technique called intra-cytoplasmic sperm injection (ICSI) can present risks to the future child.

Although egg donation is scientifically analogous to artificial insemination with donor sperm, it raises questions concerning the medical risks and potential psychological impact on the mother, couple, and future child. The risks include expense to the woman donating the egg, the increased risk of carrying multiple babies to term, and ethical and legal issues involved in egg donation that have yet to be resolved. There are many psychological, social, and economic issues associated with the use of ART.

During the course of infertility workup, attention is often focused more on the external medical team than an individual's mind and unconscious fantasy life. New infertility techniques help many infertile women to get pregnant, but the interaction between fantasy and reality stimulated by the adult wish for a baby (Pines, 1972) is complicated both before conception and during the pregnancy and entails transference feelings toward the donor egg or donor sperm.

After consultation with the reproductive physician, the couple can meet the egg donor through the donor-egg coordinator, in conjunction with the physician. Psychological issues often appear during the selection process. Some of these cases need help with the entire egg IVF treatment: donor selection, cycle coordination, egg retrieval, and transfer of embryos.

Unlike their European colleagues, reproductive specialists in the US tend to transfer multiple embryos at a time, resulting in an increased risk of multiple birth pregnancies. Although patients have opportunities to explore the concrete details of IVF in clinician offices or on websites, they often do not explore their own internal fantasy construct. One example of denial of what reality may present is dealing with multiple babies. There is potential for both pleasure and peril in carrying multiple babies to term and parenting multiples. A pre-warning educative stance could be the most crucial task of the reproductive physician and their team.

Sperm donor

Some men must confront their own infertility issue, rather than or alongside the infertility of their female partner.

In approximately 40 percent of infertile couples, the male partner is either the sole or a contributing cause of infertility. There may be abnormality related to the volume or amount, motility, or morphology of the sperm. A male fertility workup can involve genetic testing and other hormonal testing.

Treatment for male-factor infertility may include antibiotic therapy for infection; surgical correction of varicocele (dilated or varicose veins in the scrotum) or duct obstruction; or medications to improve sperm production. In some men, surgery to obtain sperm from the testes can be performed. In some cases, no obvious cause of poor sperm quality can be found. Intra-uterine insemination (IUI) or IVF may then be recommended.

When male infertility is the cause of the problem, the individual has the option of choosing a sperm donor. Intra-cytoplasmic sperm injection (ICSI)—the direct injection of a single sperm into an egg—may be recommended as part of the IVF process. In men with deformed or absent sperm, the use of this technique can carry some risks, and so the physician may recommend using a sperm donor. Insemination with donor sperm may also be considered if IUI is not successful or if the couple does not choose to undergo IVF.

Psychologically, men are not immune to devastating feelings of despair when they discover they are infertile. They might feel infertility as a loss of success—that is, as a failure or a life crisis. One of my male patients described that he felt his life come to disequilibrium. He felt a chronic sense of fear and anxiety that felt unending. Recovery from such loss may never reach full resolution.

The mourning period can linger for a long time and become an unfinished mourning in some cases. A good number of cases are unable to ask for help to process the intense feeling of disappointment and recover from the loss. The feeling of "why me?" in particular can erode one's sense of self-confidence, and self-doubt sets in.

Cases

Here, I describe three cases in psychodynamic psychotherapy that illustrate the complex psychological ramifications of infertility and the impact of ART.

Case 3: Nelly

Nelly is a thirty-two-year-old married woman who came to psychotherapy for depression. She was unhappy in her life, suffered from poor self-esteem, and harbored ambivalent feelings toward getting pregnant.

There was no history of childhood disturbances, and she was used to being an only child. She had a close, healthy attachment to her mother. Her developmental milestones were reportedly normal. She had no memory of any other caregivers besides her mother.

Unconsciously, she identified with her mother, who denigrated her stepfather. Her mother was not a nurturing woman and was often angry with Nelly when she was a young child. In contrast, her stepfather was a caring man who showed affection toward her.

As a child, she was under the impression that she was conceived out of wedlock. After Nelly turned sixteen, her mother told her that she was conceived with the help of a sperm donor. Her mother refused to tell her whether she had used a sperm bank or the sperm from a friend or acquaintance. Her world was suddenly turned upside down—not knowing anything about her origin. Her sense of identity was shaken up. Initially shocked by this tightly kept secret, Nelly became depressed when she could not find out the identity of her biological father. She was angry with her mother who had concealed the truth from her. She developed an obsession with the thought of wanting to find her biological father.

She needed to know where her chin or nose came from, and also why she developed an interest in international relations and cross-cultural psychology. She was finally able to find her father through internet research and long detective work. She wanted to solve the puzzle of "Who am I?"

Nelly hoped to forgive her mother for having her out of wedlock, and that someday her mother would tell her about the man who got her pregnant. She started to understand the anxiety her mother had had about her biological clock, and her uncertainty about her sense of femininity.

Her mother explained that she had not been sure she could marry at age thirty-four and that the clock was ticking away. She did not think she could attract a man to marry her. She decided to use an anonymous sperm donor. She said that her doctor helped her find an anonymous sperm donor. She wanted it to be something like an immaculate conception. Nelly's mother, for reasons of her own, did not tell her how she was conceived or where she found the sperm donor. She did not think that far ahead about Nelly's future inquiry into her roots. All Nelly knew was that the man she called Dad was not her biological father. None of her friends knew that Nelly had a stepfather.

Once Nelly became aware of the intensity of her chronic anger toward her mother, she decided to get psychotherapeutic help. She felt frozen in her life and could not move forward.

She was in tears one day and said that she could not free herself from her rage. "I don't understand why my mother did not think about what would happen to me when I had to live in her secret world of lies and deceit! Did she want empathy from me that she was not marriageable, and so had to resort to lying to everyone, and especially to me? I am a person too."

After Nelly discovered her biological father, she became angry with him as well. One day she related, "Now I know who the donor was I am angry with him too. It is like staying anonymous and absolved from his responsibility to finish his job! I feel miserable. My mother brought me into this world just to please herself by affirming her feminine and fertile self."

In therapy, she worked on her revived deep sense of shame and narcissistic disappointment. She was ashamed of herself and her mother, who lacked self-confidence. She had anxious fantasies that she was joined with her mother eternally and could not find her own autonomous self. She worried her rage would destroy her connection with her mother. Her fear of losing her god-like father of her childhood image of her stepfather mixed with a newly emerging image of this other "father," and these fears turned into an anxiety about her identity diffusion. She felt regret for getting herself into "this mess" without knowing how to get out of it. She wondered about repeating what her mother had done. She fantasized about staying childless to get revenge on her mother. She did not want to let technology decide her conception. She struggled with her husband's wish to have children.

She became aware of her ambivalent feelings about "motherhood" and was willing to work through her childhood wish to conceive and bear a child. She learned to value her academic achievement, which was so much greater than her mother's, without having to feel guilty about surpassing her.

Case 4: Todd

Todd and Sherry came to see me because Todd had difficulty relating to their four-year-old son. He was conceived using Sherry's eggs and sperm from a sperm donor who was a friend of the family.

Sherry was thirty-five when, after many years of trying to get pregnant, Todd's infertility was identified as the main factor in failing to conceive. Todd recalled the sense of failure that made infertility so difficult to deal with. It felt like a crisis for him, and he went through cycles of hope, fear, and despair. It felt like an emotional rollercoaster each time they started a new round of ICSI. After multiple trials, they came to accept the fact that they had to use a donor sperm. Todd wanted to use his close friend's sperm, and his wife agreed to that. When Sherry became pregnant, they were able to go through the feeling of anticipation and excitement together as a couple. The pregnancy was uneventful when their healthy baby boy was born. He was a beautiful boy who did not resemble Todd.

He found himself feeling surprised having noticed some strange feelings toward his infant son and his friend, with whom he had a close friendship and ongoing working relationship. He started to have doubts about his decision to use his friend's sperm rather than going to a sperm bank. It felt right to ask his good friend at that time, but after Sherry gave birth to their son he noticed he was having many doubts about his ability to be a good father. How could he have ignored his own longing for a biological relationship with his child? After all, many people went to Cryobank (a sperm bank) and arranged to use donor sperm. He felt his decision to ask his friend was a reasonable one at the time. He assumed the biological root did not matter and that what mattered was "the end product." He secretly blamed his wife for rushing to get pregnant. Now that their son is four years old he looks so much like his friend Peter. He avoids getting together with Peter because he worries his son will show more affinity to Peter, as well as Peter toward him.

He wondered if he could ever have the stamina to keep the secret from his son. He worried that if he disclosed to his son about his genetic roots, he would turn away from him. Did he strip from his son of the right to know who both of his parents are? How can he and his wife explain all of this to him?

He argued with himself that his son has the right to know that he is not his biological father. Furthermore, he feared that his friend Peter would someday reclaim his right as biological father. He kept wondering what would happen to their marriage when all three of them would attend gatherings, especially when they would also take their son with them. What if Sherry develops a closer connection to Peter, and consequently ends their marriage?

The new dilemma he was facing caused the two of them a lot of tension. Sherry communicated to him that it was entirely his fault that they had to resort to his friend for help. She reminded him that she had preferred an anonymous donor. They yelled at each other, and it seemed like they could not agree about anything, especially when it came down to decisions about the kind of daycare their son was to attend, or issues around discipline rules.

He recalled how he had felt mixed when there was an expectation to be a hand-holder when Sherry was going through pregnancy. He did not have time then to think through his decision, and he was expected to offer emotional support to Sherry. He did not know whether he had come to terms with his own infertility, let alone whether he was able to play a new role in supporting his wife. He did not know how he could offer support, especially when another man's sperm was involved in this process. The sense of profound failure as a male was a prevailing feeling. He was there for her when she went through the wrenching experience of the harvesting of the ova, but now he felt as if his son was a stranger. Now, in retrospect, he was able to think more deeply, and he wondered what effect his consenting to use donor sperm had had on his sense of his father identity and of his paternity rights regarding their son. He also tormented himself with another question: his fear of a seemingly weakened bond with his son. He wished he could have foreseen and prevented these psychological complications of his rushed decision.

In his therapy, Todd was able to discuss all of his many fears and self-doubts as a non-biological father, as well as his role as husband to Sherry. He felt he had to prepare himself to be less emotionally reactive or erratic when he encountered his friend. After all, he could not be ungrateful to his friend, since he was an honorable, altruist man who helped to create their son. He just could not believe that his feelings had become so out of control after the baby was born. He agreed to freeze two of Sherry's embryos for future use but he resented the thought of having more kids, fearing having to endure the same familiar range of intense emotions. The emergence of a powerful destructive fantasy was explored during this period of his work with me. How could he deny Sherry, who wanted to have more babies?

His individual therapy helped him to work through his destructive feelings, manage his intense negative affect, develop a better tolerance, and not act out on his feelings. After much individual work, he became interested in starting couple therapy. He felt he was in a much better place since developing a more consolidated sense of himself. He wanted to work on the stability of his marital relationship.

From a post-therapy contact by phone, it appeared that Todd's relationship with his son had improved and, overall, that he was able to enjoy a healthy relationship with him. He had learned the importance of openness and wanted to tell his son about the sperm donor when he was at the right age to comprehend its meaning. His son resembled him in temperament, but not physically.

Case 5: Emily

Emily, a married professional of forty-five, came to therapy because of conflicts about her desire to become a mother and marital problems. She was doubtful about their capacity to become parents.

She postponed her decision to have a child for many years and suddenly realized time was passing quickly. Emily was the second child from a family of three children. Her sister was five years older than her and was a very popular girl. She could never be like her sister, and she felt her mother preferred her sister because they were both brunette and had more in common. Emily was blonde and petite. The youngest was a girl who was born eight years after Emily. Emily grew up with a pervasive feeling that she was damaged—a feeling that was reinforced throughout her childhood by her overanxious mother. Emily was maternal toward her younger sister and fiercely competitive toward her older sister. Her father drank a lot and used foul language when he was drunk. She learned to avoid him and his abusiveness.

Emily was an obedient girl who thought she was not intelligent. Her mother constantly compared her to her older sister and her father jokingly called her "dumb little blonde." She was filled with anxiety and self-doubt. Her family was struggling financially and she felt inferior to her classmates who were living in comfort.

In her early adolescence, she befriended a girl from a high socioeconomic class. She could ride in her friend's car to school and enjoy the association with her friend's privilege of being driven by her chauffeur. She felt envious of her friend and secretly wished she could be her. Her friend's grandfather, a financially prominent man, lived with Emily's friend's immediate family. He touched Emily's chest several times inappropriately during her pubescent years. She recalled those early experiences as exciting and at the same time was fraught with shame and guilt. Her friend's move to another school put an end to it. She liked the attention the old man gave her by having her sit on his lap. She never told anyone about this.

Emily finished her high-school years and was able to enter a prestigious college. She met her husband in college and after a short few months they decided to get married. The couple waited for a few years before they decided to try to conceive.

Their trials for conception failed for a few years and finally the gynecological workup revealed multiple calcified fibromyomas in Emily's uterus. Her mother also suffered from the same problem. However, her mother had her three children before her fibromyalgia became problematic. Additionally, Emily's contributing psychological component further complicated her infertility problem. Her difficulty conceiving made her feel as though she was "damaged goods." She could not become a mother, unlike her mother and sister. She was bitter and could not accept that her uterine abnormality was an important reason for not conceiving. She felt it was not fair that her sister had children and she could not get pregnant. She was a "virtuous, good girl" and her mother relied on her when her family needed help. She felt she was denied something very important: getting pregnant like anyone else. "It was my birthright, it was not fair!," she one day uttered, and she wanted me to agree with her.

On the other hand, after she found out she could not conceive, she thought, "There was a big sign on me, like in *Scarlet Letter*, that I was *infertile*." The fertility clinic told her she needed to talk to a psychiatrist because her infertility was "psychogenic."

Patient: I was going full circle. I thought I was grieving. I was so disappointed each time I tried. My husband was not grieving. But, to be fair to him, he was very supportive of me and left me free to make a decision on how to go forward. He even was willing to be childless if I wanted to.

In one of her analytical hours, she said:

I must have made myself infertile by being neurotic. See, I am not smart enough to catch on to things quickly. See, pregnancy may never happen for me. Maybe I wanted too much like I wanted my friend's wealth and prestige. I wanted to wear expensive clothes, drive an expensive car and marry a rich man. It may be wanting everything or wanting too much. Being greedy has to do with not getting what I really want. A family is what I have always dreamed of.

She had tears in her eyes. She was in despair and full of doubt. She continued:

I did not even ask why I needed to talk to a psychiatrist. I followed their advice. Looking back, I could tell why I needed to see someone and now I am here to see you in order to understand my ambivalent feelings about motherhood.

She felt she needed me to help her to learn to accept her fate. Or maybe she would regain her stamina to pursue other options, such as using an egg donor. She had contemplated using a surrogate mother but wanted to give the egg donor option a go and her newly reconstructed uterus a good try (she had gone through extensive myomectomy). Two IVF and gamete intrafallopian transfer (GIFT) procedures had been unsuccessful. These failures had caused her great anguish, hopelessness, and self-doubt.

She realized how angry she was with her mother who did not empower her but instead had made her a damaged woman. She also felt that I was an impotent analyst and that her problem was far more complicated, beyond the scope of my expertise to be able to solve it. She was unsure about the help I could offer her. In the transference, I turned into an "infertile analyst." She agreed with my interpretation of how she wished I could have had a magic formula to help her damaged uterus, damaged mind, and damaged body. She felt I was letting her suffer in her despair and was indifferent to her pain. I emerged as a controlling pre-oedipal mother who expected total obedience and submission.

The decision to use an egg donor, and who to ask, became an obsession that agonized her for many months. She thought that maybe she could ask her younger sister to become her egg donor. She asked herself if her sister could have a second thought about going through the medical procedure. She wanted her child to have her family genes and not to go to a stranger for eggs.

After several months of deliberation, she got her courage up to ask her sister Ann to see if she was willing to be her donor. Ann was a mother of two and was happily married. She was eager to help her older sister, who she was very fond of. Emily was ecstatic when her sister accepted to be her egg donor. We tried to explore the meaning of using the eggs from her sister.

Her desire to use her sister's eggs was so strong that she was not interested in exploring the meaning of her decision. Her conscious desire was to have her family gene pool combined with her husband's sperm, rather than using some stranger she did not know. She was set to have her own child and, if her sister was willing to give her eggs, it meant that those were like her own eggs. It was like a *dress* they would both share. That is how she put it, with glee on her face. Shortly after this decision, though, she started to have fears about her sister's children, who would be her child's half-siblings. How could she bear the thought of either keeping it secret or having it out in the open?

One happy thought countering her fear was "Why not become a big, happy family?" She would carry the baby to term, and everyone would understand and support her. However, she also thought she was being greedy to ask for her sister's eggs, which were not hers. To her it was like stealing! This self-accusation led to an association with an earlier memory of her mother. She recalled how her mother asked one day how she could feed her children when there was hardly any food at home. Her father was not helping the family when he spent money on his alcohol. Food was scarce, and the family had to deal with extreme deprivation.

Together, we did a good deal of analytical work to help her with her feelings of envy and greediness, and that she would be stealing her sister's eggs. She worked hard to overcome her doubt and to move forward with her decision to enter the world of motherhood.

After this unsettling emotional period was over, a very hopeful anticipation of "becoming a mother" helped Emily to overcome her disabling doubts. Her pregnancy was uneventful and she gave birth to a healthy baby girl. She brought her baby to one of her sessions. The baby had a resemblance to her. She wanted to hear my reassurance that indeed her daughter looked like her. It was very important to her to hear it from me.

Two years later, after a hiatus in her treatment, she phoned to see me for a follow-up visit. She was caught by surprise when she began feeling confused about her reaction toward her sister at a holiday family gathering. She felt her daughter seemed to go to her aunt (her biological mother) and she imagined her sister also made it obvious through her non-verbal interaction. She told me that she had never thought about future encounters and these unexpected emotional reactions. She knew her sister had not revealed to her own two children about having volunteered to be an egg donor to her older sister. Emily was not prepared to talk about it with her daughter and was not sure that she would ever want to disclose it to her.

There was more work for us to do in therapy, exploring the meaning of her motivation toward "the promise of anonymity." She felt competitive toward her sister, and inferior to her. She struggled with the old feelings about her body that betrayed her.

Discussion

For men like Todd, infertility does not directly affect their traditional and gender role, although it can be profoundly disappointing and experienced as performance failure and a failure of masculinity. In some cultures, masculinity is directly linked to being able to produce children, and a woman's value to a man is diminished after her childbearing ends at menopause. There is no parallel to the visible personal bodily changes that the woman experiences during pregnancy.

Both men and women go through the physical and emotional turmoil of infertility. Infertility is both unique and complex. Although children are born using ART, the emotional impact of such reproductive methods needs further study. The experience of going through fertility workup and ultimately having to go through many medical and psychological phases is unique for everyone. It can be a lonely and private experience for both men and women. It affects their sense of who they are and who they imagined in their youth that they wanted to be. The fundamental value of a capacity for creation has been so deeply rooted in the sense of the bodily self that fertility challenges individual belief systems about her or his identity. The patient will struggle consciously and unconsciously with the meaning of borrowing eggs or sperm from other living beings, and with the intense emotions that erupt while they go through reproductive procedures. Analysts and psychotherapists who offer a holding environment at such trying times are critical.

Each of these cases presents a complex of social, familial, and cultural unconscious and conscious elements that in turn influence the ways in which the patient navigates through the turmoil of their development challenges and unexpected losses. Earlier unconscious conflicts reappear and affect their sense of identity and their couple relationship.

CHAPTER 4

Immigrant mothers[4]

Immigration is a complex biopsychosocial process with the capacity to mobilize the destabilization of the psychic structure, which can profoundly influence identity formation (Akhtar, 1994, 1999). Destabilization is a gradual process, and resiliency will be required to restructure the ego and reestablish an optimal psychic equilibrium.

The immigration experience affects identity development throughout the life cycle (Akhtar, 2004), especially during the separation-individuation phases of infancy, adolescence, and adulthood. Immigrant mothers, in particular, carry the shadow of their former lives within their newly found identities in their host countries (Mann, 2004). The nature of a mother's past life in her homeland, combined with the slow but steady change in identity as an immigrant, creates a complexity of experience that involves language acquisition, polyglotism, and other cultural variants—factors that significantly influence identity formation among all immigrants, but particularly among immigrant mothers. (Amati-Mahler [1995] describes polylinguism as the acquisition of various languages in childhood. Polyglotism is learning a language later in life, based on translation.) These influences, in turn, affect the separation-individuation processes of their children in the new

---

4 Originally published as Mann, M. (2016). The role of an immigrant mother in her adolescent's identity formation: "Who am I?" *The American Journal of Psychoanalysis,* 76(2): 122–139. https://doi.org/10.1057/ajp.2016.9. Reproduced with permission.

country. The immigrant mother's secure base is lost, and, if the cultural assimilation becomes complete, a newly found secure base is reborn and reconstructed.

On an internal level, the immigrant mother fluctuates between extremes of distance from her native self-representation and her newly emerging self-representation as a resident of the adopted country. The struggle in self-identity formation becomes a complex process since the immigrant mother must negotiate her own physical and psychological separation from her infantile object to stabilize her adult experience of parenthood and adapt to a new culture and language. This, in turn, influences her changing conceptualization of self and other in her individuation process.

Failure to successfully negotiate the distance between these self-representations can result in two problematic outcomes of identity (Teja & Akhtar, 1981): ethnocentric withdrawal and counter-phobic assimilation. As Winnicott (1965) described, "false" and "true" selves, alternating phases of closeness and distance from one or the other culture, may intensify the splitting of the self and the object world.

Unlike mature adults, adolescents do not have the inner stability to support appropriate levels of impulse control, because they are in the process of integrating their standard of conduct. Adolescents normally look to parents to prevent them from letting their impulses get out of control. They look to their parents to keep their impulses from overwhelming them.

The immigrant mother struggling with her own sense of identity formation is not emotionally available to help her adolescent children with the assistance they need to deal with and be able to create a sense of mastery over their anxiety.

Adolescence is a massive upheaval, characterized by fluctuations between regression and progression, dependency and self-reliance, passivity and activity, control and submission, and gender issues related to being male or female. The organizations of the ego, id, and superego lessen, and, when this is accompanied by immigration to a new country, it could potentially create sets of new outcomes for the adolescent (Mehta, 1998).

The immigrant mother, on the other hand, shaped by the influences of her child's transformation into adolescence, and by loss of power at home, as well as in her new social world outside her family life, faces a sense of incompetency on many levels, especially in relation to the acquisition and use of a new language. A lack of competency in the newly acquired language, and fear of having to replace their culture of origin with an unfamiliar new culture, bring about mourning for the loss of her symbolic, original mother tongue. Thus, her adult individuation process becomes affected or even delayed. This can lead to an intense awareness of her loss of parental authority. This mandates the enlisting of defenses and coping mechanisms in order to help her adapt to the two co-existing, contradicting, and contrasting worlds of languages, customs, mores and landscapes. Having to give up part of one's sense of individuality creates intra-psychic tension, which taxes the mother's ego structure.

Language

The immigrant's native language is the most trustworthy link to the maternal attachment figure and the culture in which she was nourished and raised. The mother tongue is a link to the earliest maternal imago. The new language may not be valued and is possibly marred with ambivalent feelings, depending on the circumstances of migration. If migration is forced, as in the case of an exile, the ambivalent conflict may be more prominently expressed.

The immigrant moves in and out of two linguistic worlds: an obliged distancing from the mother tongue and, in a parallel way, an obliged entry into a foreign land of new and unfamiliar-sounding words. Constant navigation between these two worlds adds to the splitting of self-representation. The fear of losing one's familiar linguistic world and the fear of not being able to take ownership of the new, acquired language, because of one's ambivalent feelings, makes the reconciliation of these two worlds more challenging.

Adopting a new language in a new land can present a threat to self-identity and can disrupt the inner maternal representation of the mother tongue. Inner maternal conflict regarding language acquisition in the new country brings about a loyalty conflict both in mothers and their adolescent children, which in turn impacts their relationship. If the immigrant mother perceives the new language as a threat to her maternal bonding with her adolescent child, she might unconsciously reject it or make a hostile attack to lacerate the new language. She might feel as if she is being replaced by a new, imaginary stepmother for her child.

Constantly being spoken to in a language other than one's mother tongue can be burdensome to the immigrant mother, especially when there is a lack of emotional refueling.

Some adolescent children who do understand their mother's native tongue, yet cannot converse in that language, respond in English. This may widen the gap in the mother–child dyad. The resolution of splitting the self and the object world requires a robust affect regulation, a good-enough capacity for mentalization, a holding on to social affiliation, and a reasonable passage of time for healing.

Self-identity and cultural identity

The strength of an immigrant mother's self-identity and cultural identity before migration has a great impact on her resiliency and capacity for adaptation to the new culture. Mothers with an unstable pre-immigration personality structure are at greater risk of transgressing and regressing into identity dissolution in the face of life's challenges. They have more difficulty tolerating their loneliness in the new land without extended family and social support.

Furthermore, mothers who themselves have not achieved the psychic capacity for their mid-life separation-individuation process have greater difficulty when their adolescents reach their own need to emancipate psychologically. The transformation of children into adolescents and young adults, and their separation-individuation processes, impact their mother's individuation. Through a mourning process, the mother would let go of youthful aspects of the self and replace them with the realization that a mid-life self can bring about greater autonomy and competency.

The term " separation-individuation" (Blos, 1967) refers to adolescent transition, moving from close ties to the parent to the newly, more autonomous self. It has also been applied to physical migration. The adolescent may attempt to disengage from his or her mother due to the threat of merging with her. Thus, the adolescent alternates between approaching and moving away from the mother, as well as between idealizing and devaluing her. This back and forth can pose a greater threat to the immigrant mother's intra-psychic separateness.

The new identity of an immigrant mother who does not have pre-immigration character-structure problems becomes consolidated into a reconstructed ego identity involving unconscious identification with the new culture. These newly borrowed identifications become integrated with the old, inherited culture of the country of origin.

The immigrant mother with a fragile pre-immigration ego identity is prone to be fragmented, partial, and multiple identities, leading to identity diffusion. There seems to be elasticity in the emerging expression of a hybrid identity in certain psychosocial settings, where one or the other self-identity appears to be prominent. Searles' (1986) view supports this notion that a healthy identity does not possess a monolithic solidity.

Loss and mourning

The maternal immigrant faces cultural shock and numerous losses and mourns for what was left behind. She mourns the loss of familiar surroundings, the presence of loved ones, familiar food, and customs, and, perhaps most importantly, the familiar cadence of her mother tongue. Feelings of guilt, anxiety, and fear are mixed with her mourning. The mourning process causes a serious disequilibrium in the individual's identity. The intra-psychic turmoil is a vestige of the second individuation process of adolescence (Blos, 1967). Survivor guilt over having left family members and fellow citizens behind, the anxiety over the anticipated loss of her long-held value system, and the fear that she will be viewed as a misfit within the new culture are all dominant.

Once the mourning process moves toward liberation, with the help of therapeutic intervention and social support, the mother becomes emotionally available to make a progressive move toward autonomy and identity consolidation. The mourning–liberation process of immigration results in a reconsolidated, hybrid identity in individuals who are resilient and have good-enough adaptive self and object representations.

There are many questions one can ask: What does the new culture offer to immigrant mothers, and at what cost to their cultural identity? How do they adapt to the American cultural myth, for example, and the individuality of the American character, perhaps so foreign to their own? It is of clinical interest to observe these mothers who navigate their identity dissolution and the building of a new cultural identity. Insulation and loneliness are inevitable outcomes when immigrant mothers strive to preserve the culture and language of their motherland in the new host country. These important issues lend themselves to other possible psychoanalytic technical dimensions relevant to our work as psychotherapists and psychoanalysts.

Sense of belonging

Immigration challenges one's sense of belonging in the host country. The sense of isolation and loneliness is interrelated with the sense of belonging. Living in the hope of someday returning to one's country of origin impedes the mourning process and the newcomer's assimilation into the foreign culture. The immigrant deals with his or her perspective of the past—alive in the present—without a clear boundary formation.

The clinician must be aware of the profound significance that linguistic differences play in the therapeutic and psychoanalytic setting. These differences play an important role in the psychological outcome of the analytical process with immigrant populations. Lack of sensitivity to them can cause mis-attunement, lack of understanding, or misunderstanding of cultural nuances in the therapeutic dyad, and can further traumatize immigrants.

The analyst working with an immigrant population also faces complex identity transformation issues in the therapeutic dyad. It means that, in doing analytical work with immigrant populations, the analyst inevitably goes through a re-working of his or her own identity structure. This has important counter-transference implications, which are beyond the scope of this chapter.

The case of Jason, an adolescent, indicates how the shadow of an immigrant mother's past maternal identity, and her multiple cultural identities, influenced her son's self-identity formation. Different challenges arose during Jason's various developmental stages.

Case: Jason, an Iraqi-American adolescent

The family doctor referred Jason, a seventeen-year-old, for treatment of depression and performance anxiety. In our first session, he said, "I feel I am smothered by my parents, especially my mother. When I am around them, I feel down, short-tempered, miserable, and terrible. My whole life should be focused on school only. That is what they expect of me."

Jason's parents initially contacted me through their family physician because they knew I was Persian and spoke Farsi, the language of their childhood. They also knew I could not speak

Arabic, a language that they spoke as their mother tongue. They believed I would understand their cultural expectations and their Assyrian-Iraqi background far better than other doctors.

Background

Jason's grandparents, on both sides of his family, migrated from Iraq to Northern Iran as young couples. Both of Jason's parents were born in Iran and have been friends since childhood. In their initial evaluation sessions, they relayed fond memories of their motherland, and of their tears, confusion, and upset when they had to leave. At the age of eight, Jason's mother and her family were suddenly uprooted from their familiar surroundings. Without explanation, they moved to Iraq, where they continued to live for almost two decades. Jason's father's family followed their friends' family to Iraq, where Jason's parents both earned degrees in architecture, and ultimately married each other. Their families were very supportive of their union since they had a long history together.

The young married couple decided to migrate a third time, this time to the United States. By this time, both were professionals in their twenties and left Iraq by choice, not out of political or economic necessity. They settled in Atlanta, Georgia, where Jason and his two younger sisters were born, and they then moved to the Bay Area in northern California—their fourth migration. The landscape and climate of northern California reminded them of the coastal region around the Caspian Sea in Iran, the motherland of their early childhood.

Jason's mother tried hard to be a perfect mother—an unattainable ideal. She paid a good deal of attention to her children's physical health and social interactions with their peers. She herself was raised with the help of an extended family and good social support. However, she had to raise her own children without any extended family, by herself, in a foreign country.

Jason had two younger sisters, ages twelve and eleven. The elder sister was born when Jason was four years old. In an early session, he recalled his mother coming home from the hospital with a bundle in her arms—his new sister. The following year, another baby sister was added to the family.

Early childhood

In his preschool years, Jason was afraid of the dark and anxious about his mother's safety. Upon entering kindergarten, he displayed separation anxiety and fear that his mother would forget to pick him up at the end of his school day—behavior his parents believed he would grow out of. His mother also had panic attacks over the thought of losing her children—particularly Jason to kidnappers.

Jason's IQ was tested at the beginning of kindergarten. Due to his superior intelligence, he was able to skip kindergarten and move directly into the first grade. In elementary school, he proved himself a good student, but his parents expected him to be excellent.

He was not allowed to have sleepovers or stay at a friend's house, and this turned into a major source of tension. On Halloween, Jason was not allowed to go trick or treating with his friends for fear of him getting poisoned with candies. His mother's paranoia was at its height on this specific holiday.

Adolescent years

Jason was allowed to play clarinet in the school band and was on the basketball team. His family supported his athletic abilities by driving him for three hours each way to another city, so he could play on the team. Jason had a few good friends, whose parents were also immigrants. His effort to make friends with Anglo-American children was faced with maternal disapproval. Jason had many clashes with his mother over familial rules and expectations. He wanted to be like other children. He did not want to be reminded by his mother that his ethnic background was superior to others. This notion was confusing for Jason, who wanted to blend in with his friends, not stand out among them.

Historically, Jason had been a good student, but he failed several courses in his freshman year of high school. He was interested in girls but knew he had to hide his sexual attraction from his family, especially his mother who was not familiar with the concept of dating in this country. She grew up in a culture where dating was non-existent. Young girls and boys would go out as a group to social or sports events, but never would a young man and woman go out as a couple. Marriages were primarily arranged, and dating was a much more serious proposition, with an implication that a marriage proposal would soon occur.

In high school, Jason's best friend invited him to sleep over at his house. Once again, his mother prevented him from doing so. She believed this would be culturally unacceptable. Jason began to rebel against his parents' authority and expressed his anger by neglecting his grades. It was at this juncture with his academic failure that his parents sought my help.

The initial therapeutic process

In our first session, Jason complained angrily about being smothered by his mother. He reported that she monitored him closely and insisted that he should be an obedient son.

He told me that his father had finally accepted his son's interest in studying international relations since he did not want to follow his father's career path as an architect. This was an important message to me. Jason had his own separate interests and did not want to abide by his father's wishes. He felt angry with his parents for rejecting his desire to enroll in a summer program at a prestigious university out of state, insisting instead that he live at home and attend a nearby school for the summer.

After four months of twice-weekly psychotherapy and twice-monthly parent counseling sessions, I recommended four-times-weekly psychoanalysis for Jason. His parents' reaction was an enormous shock. They interpreted this recommendation as a sign of their parental failure. However, they were willing to give therapy for Jason a try, with the understanding that he and I had only one year to work together before he entered college.

The course of analytic treatment

Jason's analytical work with me began as a struggle around how he was being transported to my office by his mother for appointments. He found me helpful when he came twice weekly, but at four times a week he began to see me as someone who was controlling his life, just like his mother. He became angry with me and threatened to stop coming to our sessions. At the same time, however, he was curious about my background and my life in the United States.

Transference

Jason engaged with me in an intense transference relationship that contained both oedipal and pre-oedipal levels of conflict, displaying both aggressive and sexual elements. The consistent interpretation of defense in the context of the supportive parental work I provided allowed him to be more mature in his use of less primitive defenses, and to articulate his feelings with insight.

I knew Jason's analysis would be interrupted when he moved away to attend college, and that our time was limited. I reminded him that it mattered what opinion he expressed in our decision to continue our work together as we had done in the past. He had friends whom he felt were untroubled and high achievers. He was happy to excel in high school and hoped he would be admitted into a prestigious university upon graduation.

Jason raised many questions about his parents and wondered why they could not become more assimilated into American culture, as he imagined that I was. He knew his parents' migration history and noticed their visible comfort and relaxed demeanor when they spoke with someone of their linguistic and cultural background. On one occasion, Jason became furious that I was not sharing my life history. He felt it was not fair that he told me all about his life without knowing much about mine. When I suggested that we needed to figure out what was so upsetting to him, he immediately responded:

You know my mother shows her mixed feelings about having left her country and living here in the States, and I can tell that she is upset, having left her own country that she misses very much. You have not told me what was it like for you when you first arrived. You don't seem to have this trouble like my mom.

When I suggested that perhaps he was worried his mother's ambivalence would turn into his own ambivalence about coming to see me, Jason nodded. Furthermore, he worried that his mixed feelings would make the good trust we had built together go away, and that would make him upset and confused. Perhaps he felt unsure if I would be able to help him with his "scary, big angry feelings" toward his mother, and toward me.

Jason was unconsciously testing maternal object representation with his newly formed developmental object, the analyst. How well could he integrate both of these object representations in the face of maternal ambivalence was my question and remained to be seen. How Jason would discover his own individuality and sense of self-identity with his natural talents and abilities, in order to better integrate his ego function, was another big question on my mind.

Role reversal and translator role

During my weekly parental work with the mother, I realized that she had many conflicted feelings. Her anxiety, guilt, and shame had roots in her cultural imperatives and her deeply held fear that her competency as a mother was sorely deficient in the context of her new environment. Her anxiety was rooted in her inability to communicate with her children in a distant and borrowed language. She feared losing her status as their parental authority. She had to rely on her children, especially Jason, to translate in many social situations in which she could not comprehend what was being communicated. Furthermore, she was ambivalent about learning American English and eventually becoming a polyglot who could easily slip in and out of her three language worlds.

The role reversal that can occur between teenagers and their parents is an important phenomenon in immigrant families, with root causes partly connected to language and custom acquisition. Jason had mixed feelings about being the translator in his family. He regularly faced situations where his mother was not able to make sense of what she heard while shopping, or visiting her children's school, and in a host of other social situations. On the one hand, Jason felt burdened. But, on the other hand, he felt elevated to a superior position of parental authority, beyond his actual capability of being an adolescent. He felt more like a parent or a teacher in comparison with his mother. This change in Jason's status occurred more frequently when he was with his mother, for his father played the traditional role of reliable provider, spending most of his time at work with his fellow coworkers and friends.

Immigrant mothers and identity formation

Among many interwoven themes that emerged during Jason's therapy, one in particular centered on his cultural- and self-identity. This is only one part of our work that reflects his struggles pertaining to the role his mother played in his identity formation.

Since their arrival in the United States, Jason's parents have remained ethnocentric and devalued American culture as being too independent and "wild." They attributed much of Jason's behavior to the American way of life and criticized him for this. His desire to connect with his peer group, many of whom belonged to other cultural backgrounds, provoked parental disapproval. His parents' rules and expectations were inconsistent with those of Anglo-American teenagers, as well as of his peers who came from other immigrant households.

Jason felt confused, for he did not know which group of friends would meet his parents' approval. He described many fights with his mother and particularly his father over this issue. He also argued with his sisters, who were beneath him in family status. His mother believed it was her duty to be a perfect mother and protect her children from "bad American influences." She was unaware of her boundary issues and intrusiveness. She would call Jason every hour, wanting to know where he was and whom he was with.

In his work with me, Jason felt free to express his political ideas and sociological stance in regard to the United States and his parents' country of origin, Iraq. He had heard stories about Iraq and Saddam Hussein's cruelty to his people because, as Kurdish minorities, Jason's parents had immigrated because they were afraid of staying in a war-stricken country should the regime change hands. They vocalized disdain toward the country's ruler and recalled how they had planned to leave Iraq before living there became impossible.

Jason's family supported the war against Saddam's regime. Initially, Jason had some fear that I would have anti-war sentiments. However, over time, he became confident I would support his ideas. Initially, he believed that, if he spoke seriously and convincingly, with passion, he would be able to influence me and change my mind. This had a familiar ring. I told him I believed that he wanted to change my opinion about the war just as he wanted to convince his father about his interest in international relations. In fact, he was quite certain that his conviction would persuade me.

Jason made multiple attempts to choose a love object in order to separate himself from his close ties with his mother. In particular, he felt that a relationship with a certain young girl, whom he used in a developmental way, would create the desired separation. The girl, however, met with his parents' disapproval. They insisted that if Jason were ever to go out with her, or think of marrying her, he would face their disapproval. His parents made it clear that a relationship with a girl who did not come from his ethnic background was not an option for him. He knew that his parents would push him toward a Kurdish union in the future. He also realized that he needed to examine his ambivalent feelings about his mother and his fear of his father's aggression.

Although Jason admired his father, he was afraid of his father's temper. His solution was to spend more time in the company of his mother and avoid talking to his father. This was a familiar theme from his oedipal period, when he showed a desire to be with his mother and resented the presence of his father and later the newborn sister. The re-emergence of the oedipal theme in Jason's adolescent phase was significant. The earlier developmental anxieties of the phallic-oedipal phase once again reappeared in this treatment phase.

The experience of accent

Jason understood the Kurdish language but could not speak it in an articulate way. He was the translator of his mother's emotional and language worlds. He had never objected to his role as translator in his family, even though he often felt burdened by it.

In one of his later sessions, Jason shared his feelings about his parents' accent. He reported that, whenever he invited a friend over to his house, he secretly hoped his mother would be out shopping with her friends. I suggested that, because he speaks fluent English, when he hears his mother's accent a discontinuity is created in his mind, as if he senses discordance in the flow of their conversational interaction.

Jason also expressed concern over the way his conversations with his mother may have sounded to his friends. I reminded him that he knew I also have an accent, and earlier he had been curious about the country from where I had emigrated. He replied that when he had asked about my accent in an early session, I made him guess. That same evening, he reported, he had asked his mother where I was from, and she told him. After that, he stopped asking about my accent.

Cultural differences

Jason enumerated multiple areas of cultural gap between his parents' culture and that of the American families he'd come to know. His sensitivity in identifying differences in the outside world extended in a parallel way to his ability to recognize differences between his thoughts and feelings and those of his mother. In the middle phase of his analysis, Jason expressed a wish that his mother would allow him to be different and not expect him to be the kind of son who has views identical to hers.

I pointed out that he was keen about our differences too, especially now that he was moving closer to the end of our work. I added that he knows he has his own sense of agency and separateness, which is different from his mother and me. I added that he is also worried that, if he becomes too separated from her, he will lose his mother's love and my caring feelings for him as well. At this point, Jason lapsed into silence, though some more, and then nodded.

As we neared the end of his second half of analysis, Jason, who was a handsome young man, began dyeing his hair even more frequently than before, to look Western. His fair skin and altered hair color gave him the illusion of being of European descent. This change in his appearance, a result of dyeing his hair, took place around the time of the attack on Iraq and again during his termination period. Jason denied experiencing anxiety over the war in Iraq. He reported that it was his father who would sit glued to the television, obsessed about all the details of the war. This was his defense against identification with his parental socio-political and ethnic identity.

The search for a consolidated ethnic identity

Jason struggled to find in his own self the ability to form a more reliable sense of self-identity. In particular, he wished for a more consolidated sense of ethnic identity but was ambivalent about identifying with his mother. Having to rely on his newly formed sense of American-ness was tenuous. Did he have a Kurdish-Iraqi part within, as did his parents, or was his identity more connected to an Anglo-American identity? At home, Jason spoke English to his parents, while they answered him in Kurdish. Although he understood most of what they said, he could not speak Kurdish. He felt left out when his parents conversed in their mother tongue.

This linguistic intimacy between his parents excluded Jason from the parental couple and initiated a re-emergence of the oedipal conflict. This old yet new version of the conflict presented Jason with a new reminder that his parents had their own separate existence and functioned as a unit in their couple relationship, while he felt like an outsider.

Jason's view of his parents' customs, language, dress, and other sociological phenomena permitted him to identify with them, and yet also made him ambivalent as to how to identify with new parental mores. His view of his struggles toward identity formation must have caused Jason inner turmoil and threatened identity diffusion, subsequently giving rise to an overwhelming anxiety. He was dismayed with their relative absence of parental influence and not maintaining more consistently a continuity of their long-held customs and values. His parents defensively adhered to an ethnocentric mode of existence, insisting that Jason would have to comply with their wishes. This was evident regarding their ideas about clothing and appearance. The parents' integration into the new host country encountered impediments of many kinds, which resulted in a sense of powerlessness, loss of status, and their own identity diffusion.

Sexual mores

Jason often felt guilty when he had to keep his attraction toward a female classmate secret. He felt even more guilt when he took the girl to a movie theater and then lied to his parents about where he had been. He told me, "If they knew about it, they would have had a heart attack!" We discussed the dilemma he was in and listed the pros and cons of revealing and concealing the news from his parents. Jason responded that once he turned eighteen his parents would no longer be able to do anything about it. Then he will be able to do what he wants with his life. Until then, however, he will have to wait. His mother's sexual mores were completely different from those in their American host country. Dating, sexual activity, or experimentation with the opposite sex did not belong to her world. It was difficult for me to discuss with his mother what is considered normal adolescent sexuality in Anglo-American culture; she was unwilling to accept it. On the other hand, it was necessary for Jason to keep his thoughts and behavior to himself and for me to keep it confidential.

Vying for control

During Jason's senior year of high school, after his acceptance into several prestigious universities, his parents decided to make plans for him to live at home and attend a nearby community college. They were convinced he would be better off under their supervision and told me they believed that he would avoid getting into drugs and drinking alcohol if he lived at home. Jason was furious with his parents' decision. He felt his mother was controlling him and this was her way of feeling empowered and regaining her lost status. After many sessions with Jason's parents, they agreed to support their son's desire to attend a university a few hours away and live in the dorm. Although my work with Jason was time-limited, he had the benefit of four-times-weekly psychotherapy for one year, and he made good, observable developmental gains. It is hard to know where he would be had he not entered treatment. Both Jason and his family were hopeful, open-minded, and motivated.

Conclusion and discussion

Jason's case presents us with several important aspects of the immigrant mother's identity and cultural values and their influence on his identity formation as he goes through various stages of development and psychic reorganization.

The influences of the language, self-identity, loss and mourning, and a sense of not belonging in a new host country are important factors that impact, in a parallel process, both the psychic structures of the immigrant mother and her adolescent child's separation-individuation and oedipality. His journey through various phases of his developmental migration presents a challenge for his necessary, age-appropriate adolescent transformative changes.

Adolescents emigrate from the family and move into a world of freedom, supposedly functioning autonomously at the end of the latency period. The developmental and psychological migration of an adolescent is important in order to establish an optimal distance from the mother and achieve completion of his individuation. At the same time, the psychic equilibrium of the immigrant mother is affected by the new host country's expectation that she be able to acculturate without delay. If the cultural settings of the host country are hostile or traumatizing, they can adversely affect the psychological equilibrium of the mother.

The integration of maternal ambivalent feelings is particularly crucial, because the immigrant mother struggles to resolve her own ambivalence in order to offer her ego strengths to her adolescent child. She will have to help him or her further to resolve developmental conflicts during this phase of adolescence. Her ambivalence might be pervasive but, as seen here, is particularly noticeable by how often she uses the new language and how frequently she reverts to using the mother tongue.

Adolescent progressive and regressive experiences and incorporation of the maternal cultural and ethnic upbringing become more exaggerated. Thus, the adolescent has a much more difficult task of reconciling identification with his immigrant mother. The adolescent's task becomes even more daunting when the mother is struggling to solidify her own sense of multicultural identity, having to overcome her ambivalence. The mother may experience the distancing of her child as more of a threat during the second rapprochement phase of adolescence. The threat to her ego integrity could prevent her from being fully present to help her child's ego strengths and identity integration. Thus, both the mother's and the child's newly acquired self-representations, as well as their old self-representations of mother and child, can become more vulnerable and subject to fragmentation during this process.

A mother and her son's respective developmental lines intersect and influence one another. The mother's projections of her self-representation onto the adolescent can increase the internal conflict of an already troubled sense of newly acquired American identity, as well as her previous, yet present and living, ethnic identity. Establishing a sexual identity, as part of an overall self-identity, can present conflicts as well.

If the immigrant mother has conflicts around her child's sense of loyalty to the host country and her own dis-identification with American culture or language, then the individuation process and formation of intimacy outside of the family setting can become even more problematic. Furthermore, the establishment of mastery and control over libidinal and aggressive drives by means of restructuring the psychic apparatus (including the ego, superego, and the ego ideal) can present difficulty for the adolescent. Additionally, the final resolution of the Oedipus complex, in both positive and negative aspects, facilitated by temporary regression to an earlier level of conflict in the adolescent phase, would not be without significant psychological repercussions. The final task of genital primacy for adolescents also becomes complicated if the immigrant mother is unable to deal with her ambivalent feelings about new customs, language, sexual mores, and a lack of integration between ethnic identity and newly acquired self-identity.

As Peter Blos suggests in his paper "The second individuation process of adolescence" (1967, p. 163), the mandatory part of normal development, in which there is a re-working during the adolescent phase of the early separation-individuation process of the first three years of life, would find a new opportunity to work through a second individuation process, providing the parents have resolved their own conflicts. Parental prohibition, however, can prevent the adolescent from forming peer–object relationships and hinder the individuation process by way of separating the adolescent from their intra-psychic infantile object ties and dependencies. The process of separating from maternal ties and turning to group affiliation can therefore become problematic. The regressive and progressive processes accompanied by both depressive affects at the loss of earlier object ties and exhilaration at the development of independent autonomous functioning would be compromised. Adolescents cope with the anxiety and depression created by this process either by withdrawal and inactivity or by motor activity, which may take on frantic proportions in their efforts to escape loneliness and boredom. The ambivalence of early object relations reappears in this phase. The adolescent ego finds the ambivalence intolerable, and it will lead to defensive operations of negativism, oppositionalism, and indifference.

Some adolescents act out their immigration neurosis by rebelling against parental, social, and cultural values. (I define "immigration neurosis" as an internal conflict associated with being an immigrant, displaced person, or refugee, similar to "traumatic neurosis" or "war neurosis".) Such adolescent rebelliousness has a particular quality of intense forcefulness. It carries with it earlier roots of their unresolved mother–child dyadic conflicts, mis-attunement, and possible attachment disruptions. When the mother's value system within the nuclear family clashes with her adolescent child's value system, the psychological emancipation of the adolescent becomes strained.

Adolescents, in their strong fantasy framework, strive to belong to their new peer group. Parents do not belong to their world, particularly when immigrant parents present a variety of different social and cultural values that are discordant with contemporary culture. Jason's case suggests that both positive and negative aspects of ethnic identification became diluted during his adolescence, while identification with parental mores must have taken place at the same time. In addition, his mother's mourning process at the start of her migration left Jason with unfinished internal work from his first separation-individuation process.

Because of his mother's many migrations and her own mid-life separation-individuation issues, Jason's second, or adolescent, separation-individuation process was delayed too. His oedipal phase was also affected, due to residual, unresolved pre-oedipal conflicts and an unfinished first separation-individuation process. His fear of being overpowered and controlled by his mother, his aggressive impulses toward her, and his castration anxiety were the central features of his turmoil. His father, who was not his ally, contributed to his low self-esteem and lack of confidence. His father's loss of status and the absence of cultural support weakened him in Jason's eyes.

Jason's analysis and my parental work with his immigrant mother illustrate an important point: working with an immigrant population requires accommodating the therapeutic framework to cultural differences, assuming the role of a developmental object, and conducting the developmental work to facilitate the individuation process. In working with these types of patients, the analyst can encounter higher degrees of complexity involving a modified analytic technique, special concerns with transference and counter-transference dilemmas, and the need for a more sensitive attunement to cultural and language differences.

PART II

CHILDHOOD

CHAPTER 5

Childhood abuse: Abused children and their abusing families

Child abuse is described as reaching an epidemic proportion. It is a serious problem in North America, Europe, Asia, Africa, and Australia. In fact, it is a global problem. A mobilization of national concern and resources had begun in the US in 1975 to alleviate child abuse, which reached a turning point. The problem of child abuse has its roots in ancient history. Still, it did not receive widespread public recognition until 1962, when a "Battered Child Syndrome" description entered the media.

Violence inflicted on children was viewed as a public health problem that affected family members, parents, and children. The Child Abuse Prevention Act had been signed into law, the National Center on Child Abuse and Neglect was in operation, and the National Committee for Prevention of Child Abuse had been established. For the first time, the federal government made long-term grants of millions of dollars available to programs designed to prevent child abuse, identify cases, and alleviate the consequences to the families of abused children by effective intervention. Many states have launched public education campaigns to encourage the reporting of suspected cases of abuse and the detection of early signs of child abuse.

These new changes have been significant compared to what previously has been, but we need to do so much more, and so much remains to be done in all aspects of this universal problem. I feel we have barely made a dent in the child abuse problem, especially with abusing parents. Primary prevention programs to keep abuse and neglect from happening are few and, in some areas of our world, non-existent. The focus on the treatment of abusing parents and preventing them from repeating the abuse and neglect are not adequately researched and evaluated in most of the world.

We cannot just punish the parents and place the children in foster homes. Legal, medical, and mental-health professionals are generally holding a pessimistic view about abusing parents. They see them as beyond help since they are seen as repeating the abuse as they were subjected to the abuse themselves, what was done to them, and what they do to their children, turning passive into active or identifying with the legacy of their past abuse. There has not been an effective way to prevent and treat such cases, and there has been limited success in doing individual dynamic psychotherapy or rehabilitating parents who abuse their children.

I want to emphasize the system nature of child abuse so that the root cause and the applied therapeutic interventions can be properly understood and appropriately designed. Before I discuss the system approach, I want to go over the impact of child abuse on the child's attachment system.

Abuse by an attachment figure undermines the very existence of the child's psyche. Evidently, for every human being, the preservation of self-continuity has the highest evolutionary priority. The two highest priorities for all living organisms are to preserve the psyche's coherence and the capacity for agency. Abuse is an assault that fragments the psyche in terms of its functions; parent is not supposed to harm their children intentionally. Mothers are more likely to abuse children than fathers. One study shows that the rate of child fatalities in the hands of mothers is much higher statistically. The child is unable to reconcile psychologically the image of the loving mother with their experience of an abusive mother. It is not only because the child cannot mentalize, but also if he does so, he cannot comprehend how it could be that his mother/parent wanted to hurt him. Therefore, the need to split off the terrifying experiences is devastating.

Abuse makes the child helpless and unable to defend himself or to make any appeal to the abusing parent. Therefore, there is an intense sense of terror that spikes high and makes the child psychically paralyzed. The combination of the inability to comprehend and the inability to act often leads to a sense of helplessness and failure. The abusive parents shatter the child's belief in a safe family environment and his external world. The child believes the parent must be correct in their perception that he is terrible. It is not uncommon for abusive parents to blame their child for being wrong.

Abuse evokes anger in the child, which has to be kept hidden. The experience of anger confirms the child's badness. The strong attachment bond leads to the idealization of a parent. The child tries to please the parent actively and splits off the unintegrated rage, terror, and helplessness. When the bond is weak, the child may act out his rage as a defense against the split-off helplessness experienced at the hands of the abuser and against oneself.

In the treatment of abused children, psychoanalysts can help the abused child by assisting the child in making sense of the parent's abusive behavior. It can become an important focus to help the child develop and maintain a sense of continuity in his own psychic coherence and agency. Aside from the early precursors for abuse, parental lack of capacity to provide a secure attachment, and parental psychopathology, for many additional reasons, we ought to look at child abuse requiring to be viewed as a systems approach.

First, the entire family is often involved in child abuse, not just the mother, father, or other caretakers who are interested in the injuries they cause. The mother, father, siblings, and the environment— they all play a part. The interlocking development of a symbiotic relationship between spouses and their children can be understood and broken up only in a systems approach.

Second, families do not live in a vacuum, on the community level, any effort at primary prevention will have a better chance of success if the different parts that make up the system of host, agent, and environment are properly identified. Environmental stresses and community support networks are considered crucial in the outcome of any intervention.

Third, family, society, and socio-geo-political systems are all part of a single system, and what affects one will affect another. These systems are interlocking and impact one another. Our cultural scripts potentially lead parents to believe that all babies are always cute and adorable and that mothers must maintain the serenity of the Madonna; the normal frustration, anger, and resentment of mothering will spill over into violent behavior and are bound to culminate more violence against children. Therefore, violence inevitably occurs in the home. Violence in the world influences the lives of individual families throughout. Gun violence has become like an epidemic in the United States. Instant communication has made the inhabitants of the Worldwide globe always connected and yet more vulnerable to the propagation of violence. Instant communication is just one example of the rapid technological changes we all are swept up in.

Fourth and final, we see a future shock in the global community. The epidemic proportion of child abuse and domestic violence is one of the striking manifestations. Too many changes that come too fast contribute to the prevalence of child abuse.

We are aware that stress is one of the critical factors in causation; I believe that abusive families live in a relentless "life crisis" based on demanding ongoing adjustment and readjustment to a continuous and constant change. Researchers have discovered the excessive numbers and magnitude of changes that mark the lives of families twelve months before the act of child abuse. As we know, excessive change precedes the onset of illness, accidents, or injury; the evidence suggests that it is also a predisposing factor in child abuse.

Psychotherapists and other professionals who deal with abused children need to know an effective way of measuring and evaluating if and when it is safe for the child to return to the family home. We also need to do good research in figuring out how much changes as a result of therapeutic intervention the abusive parents would be able to go through to resume their role as non-threatening and non-abusive parents. The welfare of children is at stake if people would rather pretend that child abuse is not one of their concerns. In the majority of cases, some of these people have to be forced to face the fact that not only does child abuse occur frequently, but it is also a major public health problem. There seems to be a tacit agreement among many people who do not want to meddle in each other's private life matters until it becomes crystal clear and impossible to ignore the abusive behavior.

Drawing public attention to child abuse will spotlight other thorny issues that people prefer to ignore. For example, spanking and discipline are inextricably involved in the problem of abuse.

One point of view is that the line between spanking and beating is thin. Indeed, that abuse is often a spanking that simply goes too far.

Corporal punishment and how parents discipline their children will invite controversial scrutiny and national debate as the problem of child abuse becomes more of a public issue. Historically, children have been viewed as the property of their parents, and parents have the right to rear their children as they wish. As for discipline, "parents have the right to punish their child however they like." By custom, as well as by law, parents' rights are well established. This is not true of children's rights, however. Most people believe if the punishment of the child is so severe that it amounts to abuse, the child should be removed from the home only as a last resort.

Some individuals who never learned what it means to be nurtured will find it almost impossible to encourage others unless role models are provided (i.e., parents who were fortunate enough to have had good-enough mothering), which is needed to enter the homes of potential abusers and provide them with models they never exposed to in their childhood. It also means the abusers will need community support that allows them to leave their child with a good surrogate mother when there is a risk for abusive behavior. In some societies, there are parents' aides who act as surrogates. We still need to do further research on the role of church, school, and job environments in terms of support for mothers, children, and families and in terms of relieving sources of stress.

The childrearing function plays an important factor in many different societies. When biological parents are unable to or not prepared to rear their children, how can we train or make professional parents responsible for raising the children in need of surrogate parenting? Child abuse is a public health problem that requires a multidisciplinary approach, community support, and a national understanding of public health approaches. Primary prevention means reducing the incidence of new cases, meaning keeping child abuse from happening. Secondary prevention applies to keeping parents from repeating abuse through therapy and, therefore, reducing the prevalence of the problem. There are multiple definitions for child abuse. A broad view of child abuse applies to neglect and psychological abuse as well as physical abuse.

Some definitions are comprehensive in that they describe child abuse as anything that is not conducive to the child's general welfare. We can agree to the following definition: anything that is non-accidental physical injury inflicted on a child by a parent or other caretaker deliberately or in anger. Conducive to the child's general welfare. This definition encompasses the kind of abuse specified in Kempe's "Battered Child Syndrome" but only applies to the physical aspect of Silver's child abuse syndrome which includes "social" and emotional abuse as well as physical mistreatment.

Martin has noted, "Maltreatment of children is a spectrum. Physical assault, neglect, and nutritional or emotional deprivation are points on the spectrum and overlap considerably. While a broken bone can be identified by x-ray, how can we identify a mental injury?"

We need to answer these questions with specific definitions that can be agreed on and written into law. We need to refine our skills to come up with clear descriptions of circumstances and conditions under which abuse occurs.

Child neglect is also a separate problem: child abuse is an act of commission, whereas neglect is one of omission. However, the two may overlap in terms of some basic personality characteristics of abusing and neglectful parents. Gil estimates that one-third of abusive parents also neglect their children. A person who abuses has much more of an emotional investment in the child. We still ought to be able to focus on how to detect abusive families, understand the cause, and offer prevention and treatment.

The mother was reared in a way that precluded an excellent enough positive experience of being mothered and nurtured. Thus, she cannot mother or encourage her child as an adult. She exhibits a lack of trust in others, a tendency toward isolation, a non-supportive marital relationship, and excessive expectations toward the child. Potential for abuse becomes activated when the child is perceived as a "special" child, such as being seen as retarded, hyperactive, or in some other way different. In addition, a crisis or a significant stressor triggers the abuse. Stress alone does not explain the reason for child abuse. The vast majority of lower-income people do not harm their children. In this model, we see role reversal in operation. The person who abuses her child may have learned that this is the only way to relate, as an adult, to her child. We can define non-accidental physical injury to a child as any harm intentionally inflicted by a parent or caregiver, whether deliberate or out of anger, that negatively affects the child's overall well-being. The current ideas and theories on causes of child abuse relate to seven models, ranging from the psychodynamic model to the mental illness model. The earlier pioneers, such as Kempe et al., rely on a psychodynamic model of understanding the lack of "mothering imprint" as the basic dynamic of the potential for abuse.

There are also other models that other investigators use to explain the causality of child abuse. There include the "Personality or character trait model," the "Social learning model," the "Family Structure model," the "Environmental stress model," the "Social-psychological model," and the "Mental illness model."

There have been studies in which there have been more careful observations of mothers and their children have found a more vital link between having been abused in childhood and being an abusive parent. In a survey of such studies, Joan Kaufman and Edward Zigler, psychologists at Yale, concluded that 30 percent is the best estimate of the rate at which abuse of one generation is repeated in the next.

Responses to Abuse

Denial that one has been abused is emerging as a source of trouble later in life. We can define non-accidental physical injury to a child as any harm intentionally caused by a parent or caregiver, either deliberately or out of anger, that negatively affects the child's overall well-being." Researchers find that many adults who were abused as children do not think of themselves as having been victimized. For instance, three-quarters of men in one study who described punishments that, by objective standards, constitute abuse—such as being burned for an infraction of a minor household rule—denied that they had been abused. That phenomenon is common among those who go on to become child abusers, according to Dr. Krugman, and is part of the cycle by which beat children become abusive parents.

> When you ask them if they were ever abused, they tell you, "No," …
>
> But if you ask them to describe what would happen if they broke a rule, they'll say something like, "I was locked in a closet for a day, then beaten with a belt until I was black and blue." Then you ask them, was that abuse? and their answer is, "No, I was a bad kid and my parents had to beat me to

make me turn out okay" (Goleman, 1989, quoting Dr. Richard Krugman)

While there has been much attention by psychotherapists in recent years on women who were sexually abused in childhood, a more recent focus is on men who suffered sexual abuse. Such men are much more reticent than women about admitting what happened to them and dealing with the trauma, according to Mike Lew, co-director of the Next Step Counseling Centre in Newton, Massachusetts, and author of *Victims No Longer* (2002) about the problem. Denial of having experienced abuse is becoming increasingly recognized as a factor that can lead to difficulties later in life. Researchers have found that children who have experienced abuse tend to fare better after the abuse found, when they have someone in their life—a relative, teacher, minister, or friend—who is emotionally nurturing. In helping a child recover from abuse, "you need to counteract the child's expectations that adults will be deeply uncaring," explained Martha Erickson, a psychologist at the University of Minnesota.

Among adult victims of childhood abuse who are in therapy, a common refrain from patients is that "it just wasn't that bad," said Terry Hunt, a psychologist in Cambridge, Massachusetts, who specializes in their problem. "The key to their treatment is facing the fact that their parents were so cruel to them; they've bought the parent's word that they were bad and deserved it. The damage shows up in their intimate relationships: they're waiting to get hit or used again."

One of the crucial differences between those abused children who go on to become abusers and those who do not, he said, is whether they have the insight that their parents were wrong to abuse them. Dr. Hunt finds that the most troubled among his patients are those who were told as children by adults other than their abusive parents that the abuse was justified. "If an abused child thinks, 'That was wrong, they shouldn't have done that to me—I'm not that bad,' then he can still love his parents but decide not to repeat the abuse when he becomes a parent," said Dr. Krugman. "The child somehow gets the message that what happened is not his fault, that he is not to blame."

When parents are not the abusers, how they react to its discovery is crucial. In a study of children who had been involved in sex rings, those who had the fewest lasting problems in later years were the children whose parents had been understanding of the child, according to Ann Burgess, a professor of nursing at the University of Pennsylvania Medical school. "These kids recovered with no symptoms, while those whose parents blamed them had the worst outcome." The factors that lead some children to become abusers while others become excellent parents are being revealed in research at the University of Minnesota. Psychologists there are currently studying a group of children born to parents with a high probability of becoming abusers. Not all those in the study were abused as children; they were selected instead because they were poor, single, got pregnant at an early age, and had chaotic households—all factors that correlate highly with child abuse.

In addition to physical and sexual abuse—the two varieties most often studied—the researchers are also studying children whose physical care is neglected, those whose parents constantly berate and criticize them, and those whose parents are utterly unresponsive to their emotional needs. The study is one of the few that has followed children from birth. It finds that there are different emotional effects from each of the different kinds of abuse and that these effects change from age to age. For instance, children whose mothers were emotionally cold during infancy had emotional and learning problems at the age of six that were as severe as—and sometimes more severe—those found in children whose mothers had been physically abusive but emotionally responsive during their infancy.

When the same children were studied between the ages of four and six, the most severe problems were found in those whose mothers neglected their physical care. The study also finds general effects that come from maltreatment of any kind.

"The earlier the maltreatment occurs, the more severe the consequences," said Martha F. Erickson, a psychologist at the University of Minnesota, who was one of those who conducted the study (Pianta, Egeland, & Erickson, 1989). Many of the lifelong psychological effects of abuse stem from a lack of nurturance, they conclude, a lack that lies behind all kinds of maltreatment. The Minnesota researchers report that among those abused children who go on to become abusive parents, there is little repetition of a specific type of abuse.

The following are some of the common characteristics of abusive families, although the list is not exhaustive.

Abusive families tend to look just like other families in our neighborhoods, schools, and churches when they are outside of the privacy of their own home.

One hears from the people in therapy how respected their abusive parent(s) were/are in the church and the community. This can leave survivors wondering why they were treated so badly and if the fault lies within them.

No families are perfect. No parents are perfect. In looking at the characteristics of abusive families, we are not talking about the "healthy-enough" parent who makes an occasional mistake or handles a situation in a way that causes minor offenses. We're talking about chronic, severe offenses that leave deep, lasting scars in the hearts of those who are impacted by them.

The needs of the family members are expendable. The parents must fulfill the children's needs, and other adults must meet the needs of the parents. In abusive families, the children are used to satisfy the needs of the parents while the needs of the children go unmet. Where there is favoritism, the kids' needs, seen as "lesser," can go unfulfilled while the "elevated" kids are daunted.

Reality is difficult to discern. Being at home with our families should be our safest experience. In abusive families, the place that is supposed to be the safest becomes the most dangerous. Children naturally want to believe that whatever their parents do is appropriate. We are taught to ignore our God-given discernment and perceptions by abusive parents who tell us that the abuse is a regular "expression of love" or "deserved" because of our inappropriate behavior.

The victim is made responsible. Every adult's responsibility is to take care of the children that God has entrusted them to parent and provide for. Abusive parents push their responsibilities onto their children. They may be expected to take care of the younger siblings and perform unreasonable tasks well beyond their years. Sometimes, they are expected to fulfill the sexual desires of evil parents.

The family appearance is deceptive. We have already discussed the banality of evil—the thought that most abusive people and families look very respectable to those on the outside. Abusive people can go to great lengths to maintain a "perfect" outward appearance.

The truth is ignored. Members of a dysfunctional family may be so focused on maintaining their sense of "peace and calm" that they miss apparent signs that abuse is occurring. I've worked with abuse survivors whose history of abuse was so clear that I couldn't believe that other parents had no clue that the abuse was occurring.

Family abusers use force. In some situations, abusive family members may use manipulation and grooming to gain the trust of the victims; however, the "tenderness" of the grooming process gives way to threats and force to ensure that the victim maintains the secrecy of the abuse. Other times, the perpetrators begin the abuse with aggression. Because the victims feel helpless to stop the abuse, the amount of aggression may decrease over time and may fall away altogether. Learned helplessness is when a victim is strong enough to control the abuse but is convinced that the situation is hopeless and continues to comply. This explains why many victims fail to walk away from the abuse or reach out for help, even when help is readily available.

There is no straightforward, healthy communication. Much of the communication in abusive families is intentionally confusing and manipulative. Abusers may hide behind words that have double meanings so they can quickly deny their ill intent. If they spoke clearly, the destructive motives of their heart would be evident to all.

The victim's rational response is often futile. Abusers don't respond to reason. Abusers aren't interested in the truth. They are champions of denial (refusing to admit or acknowledge the truth), projection (attributing their harmful actions and motivations to others), and blame-shifting (claiming their negative behavior was the result of the victim's actions). Abusers "twist reality" to match their world.

Power is used to exploit. In healthy families, power protects and empowers the vulnerable to reach their full potential. In abusive families, power is used to control and ensure that the weaker remain under the control of the dominant.

Some of the Abusive families are emotionally unstable. Victims often feel like they are "walking on eggshells." An action that was perfectly acceptable yesterday may trigger a violent reaction today; therefore, life is unpredictable, and one can never let down one's guard. They may also find themselves having a wide range of feelings about their abuser, who may be beating them one moment and pretending to love them by sexually abusing them the next. Victims may recognize that abusive behavior is wrong but find themselves lacking the perceived favorable attention they are receiving.

The victim is shamed, blamed, and demeaned. I've heard from many survivors that their abusers manipulated them with kindness before the sexual abuse and then verbally assaulted them unmercifully after the abuse. Some are blamed for the assaults by the perpetrators, and others claim that the abuse wouldn't have happened if they had better character or that they specifically behaved in a way to provoke the abuse.

Family members are isolated and lack intimacy. Healthy families have nothing to hide. Dysfunctional families are afraid of being found out. It is common for perpetrators and those who enable them to pull their victims away from those who can identify unhealthy behavior.

Since abusers are proficient at using, the victims quickly learn to shut off their desires.

Ironically, the perpetrators paint a picture where the world is unsafe and dangerous and that they are the only ones the victims can trust.

A strict code of silence is enacted. Abusive families follow a strict No Talk Rule. The perpetrators don't want to be found out and communicate that there will be dire consequences for anyone who tells others about the abuse.

Abusive families deny and distort healthy emotions. Children want the world to make sense. Most abuse victims believe that the abuse was their fault. Many were told so by their abusers. For an abusive world to make sense, survivors learn to embrace the idea that the abuse was their fault. This also gives victims a strange, false sense of control. Other victims were told that they were overreacting and scolded for having negative feelings about the abuse. Unfortunately, the more profound message is that they learn to distrust their healthy emotions. They either embrace dysfunctional emotions or shut them off altogether.

The wrong ones are protected. Perpetrators want to disguise their abusive system and maintain a false presence of their external appearance. They use manipulation, intimidation, and violence to achieve that goal. Those who accuse the victims are often shamed and blamed—even within their family system.

Child abuse is an ongoing issue that needs continuing research and understanding to enable us to help those who have experienced it and to create measures to prevent it for future generations.

CHAPTER 6

Shame veiled and unveiled: The shame affect and its re-emergence in the clinical setting

One of Wiley Miller's cartoons in the *New Yorker Magazine* depicted a patient who had crawled underneath an analytical couch instead of lying on it. Only his feet are showing. The analyst says, "Ordinarily, I steer clear of reaching any conclusions during a first session, but I'm guessing you are dealing with some esteem issues ..." This cartoon introduces the theme of this chapter—shame veiled and unveiled with one aspect of shame manifestation as transference shame in an analytical setting.

The topic of "shame" is an important one for clinicians mainly because it has been ignored in psychoanalysis for such a long time. As with most interests that motivate us, I became curious about my own personal experience and sensitivity to shame within an analytic framework with my patients. My interest in shame also came as a pursuit of what underlies treatment failure and impasse in psychoanalysis and psychotherapy. I discovered the absence of psychoanalytical understanding and focused discussion about shame in analytic literature before 1971. There has been relative neglect during the dominance of drive/defense psychology in traditional psychoanalytic thought. The study of narcissism and self-broadened the psychoanalytic theory and allowed the examination of a painful experience of shame, which goes beyond guilt and feelings of intra-psychic conflict.

I will devote some time to relating contemporary understanding of the affect of shame, and I will give several clinical vignettes to demonstrate the clinical manifestation of shame-related affect and shame defenses: defenses like anger and rage, contempt and envy, and depression. Kohut considered adaptive defensiveness, enabling the patient to bear the painful nature of shame. He believed that shame represents a self-object failure in mirroring, in which case shame sensitivity and anxiety will reflect concern about the detailed empathic attunement of, and attachment to, significant objects that function as self-objects.

Much of our work often involves understanding the causes of shame and its effects on our patients. There seems to be an agreement among clinicians that the affect of shame is prevalently present in its veiled and unveiled forms more in narcissistic characters as well as more structured neurotic characters.

Definition of shame

The word shame has many meanings. It is both a noun and a verb (one can feel shame, and one can also shame another). The noun refers to an emotion but is also used for the acts that precede that emotion (one can do shame). As an emotion it is complex, with important cognitive aspects and an emphasis on self-awareness.

Shame is a developmentally advanced emotion, whose boundaries with other emotions are blurred and to some extent arbitrary, heavily influenced by cultural context and linguistic convention.

The meaning of shame depends on the theoretical structure in which it is embedded.

As psychoanalysts, we are involved in constructing accounts, narratives, portrayals of our patients' lives and their experiences in treatment. Constructs center around drives, conflicts, objects, affects, anxiety, defense, guilt, shame, narcissism, tragedy, or many other themes. Each of these along with their theoretical accompaniments provides the opportunity for therapist/analysts to help patients form a new psychic structure.

Being an intense social phenomenon, shame depends on cultural context more than other affects. There are cultures based on shame in the same way that Western cultures, at least in the past, have been based on guilt.

We may be able to learn about shame both from the role of culture as well as knowledge of infant observation research.

It would be useful to distinguish between several concepts closely associated with shame and make a distinction between shame and guilt:

Shame includes an affect: a searing, painful affect accompanied by gaze aversion, a wish to disappear, a disconnection from the prevailing interpersonal process, perhaps from the social order entirely.

It also includes comportment organized around avoiding shame: in French, *Pudeur* as opposed to *Honte*, the affect itself. The obverse of shamelessness, modesty, may be a defense used against shame.

Shame can be used, in the future sense, as an anticipatory anxiety about experiencing shame, signal anxiety, or signal shame: that anticipates rejection, disgrace, ostracism, relegation to inferior status—the impending social disaster we call mortification, a topic we'll discuss later. Perhaps you recall that a few years ago, a Marine Corps General committed suicide when he felt he would be exposed as someone wearing a medal to which he wasn't entitled. Tragic, the more so, because it later appeared that he was entitled to wear that medal.

The impact of "shame" includes not merely the intensity of the affect, but the powerful workings of shame fantasies by which the experience or anticipated experience of shame is processed: paranoid shame, or the anticipation of shame coming from the deliberate mocking of contemptuous others; projective identification, often setting off reciprocal shaming as attempts to turn the tables on the shamer; and omnipotence, especially in revenge fantasies in which the avenger imagines his or her vengeful solution to the experience of being humiliated to be done in complete freedom from the consequences to self and others.

Shame is not always a negative force. The anticipation of shame can be a powerful positive motivator and socializer.

At the weaker end of the continuum there is embarrassment, referring to a less painful experience, one associated with action or exposure, often of a social nature. Humiliation is usually felt more strongly, a feeling of embarrassment at being humbled in the estimation of others, often by a specific act. Chagrin is humiliation mingled with vexation or anger. Shame, the strongest of these feelings often involves unconscious elements, associations of factors coming from infancy, childhood, or adolescence. Many times, the origins of these feelings are obscure to the individual experiencing them.

Shame is associated with feelings of inferiority or with failures to meet standards of accomplishment set by others, for instance, becoming potty trained, or by the self—successfully solving a puzzle problem. The feeling of shame is the result of moral transgressions and social blunders. Younger children associate shame with embarrassment, blushing, ridicule, and a desire to escape. Older children characterize shame as feeling stupid, being incapable of doing things right, and not being able to look at others (Ferguson, Stegge, and Damhuis, 1991).

Shame is not to be understood as an analytic bedrock more basic than guilt. Guilt has been defined as the emotion associated with having committed an offense … or wrong, especially against some moral or penal law … a feeling of responsibility for some act. Guilt is the affect experience of having committed a moral transgression—hurting another or committing a "sin."

No matter what their respective times of origin, shame dynamics and guilt dynamics are often intertwined in complex ways.

Theoretical background

It is a tribute to Freud's genius that all his many contributions to the understanding of shame have proven to be of enduring value both clinically and theoretically. There has been over a century of psychoanalytic studies regarding shame. Comparisons have been made with social and philosophical theories and contemporary views on affect. The relation of self and object in the early developmental life of infants has been studied in order better to understand "shame"

There seems to be agreement that neonates can grasp the equivalence between facial patterns of movement they see and patterns of movement they make on their own (Field et al., 1982). Infants can recognize correspondence across perceptual modalities innately because neonates can recognize the equivalences between the acts they themselves perform and those performed by adults;

they have a mechanism by which to begin identifying with other human beings, to recognize them as "like me."

Shame is closely linked with intentionality and intersubjectivity. As Lichtenberg says, "the infant is an accomplished action initiator and responder before he can achieve psychic representation of the purpose of the action or of himself as the originator of the action" (Lichtenberg and quoted in Lansky & Morrison, 1995, p. 44).

He proposes the following schema for shame as a preverbal development. Shame as an affective, non-reflective, non-self-attributive experience may be a part of the daily life of every infant.

Caregivers interrupt infants' rising interest in throwing food, biting the nipple or pulling on an earring and thus automatically trigger an affect that at least some of the time may be experienced as shame.

Shame, then may be an important aspect of the socializing of infants during the period when the sense of self is forming.

Shame inhibits interest and excitement and therefore can be considered a counterpart to affirming and confirming responses.

Whether shame as a lived experience makes a useful contribution to the regulation of undesired behaviors or results in pathological inhibitions and a lowered sense of self-worth will be determined by the frequency with which caregivers activate shame and the length of time infants are allowed to remain in a shame state before reparative efforts can occur.

The balance between affirmation/shame may be generalized from the lived experiences of the preverbal period and will influence unconscious and conscious mental states.

In each motivational system, shame may serve to foster conformity and deference to standards of conduct that are valued by the group. Alternatively, shame may be interwoven into the fabric of the developing sense of self in such a way that when shame is triggered, the developing child is vulnerable to a rapid diminution of the cycle of interest/excitement and the cycle of enjoyment/joy. Thus, the child is prone to a fragmented and depleted sense of self.

This depiction of shame in the preverbal phase is a useful schema for examining one important aspect of infancy. However, it is too linear for a dynamic system conception. The effect of any single event and stimulus, or any self and interactive attempt at regulation is highly unpredictable. The unpredictability extends to what affective response or combination of affect responses may occur and how vulnerable the baby and the dyad are to the problematic effect of the response. Attachment research confirms that initiative may well be preserved in the secure infant. Who readily seeks the safety of a secure base and readily enters into exploratory activity. Likewise, initiative may be highly conflictual in the ambivalently attached infant, blunted in the avoidant infant, and chaotic in the disorganized infant. The problematic shame is implicated in insecure attachment and especially in the patterns of the avoidant infant.

As symbolic play and verbal communication comes online after 18 months, the self-attributive nature of shame becomes a factor that can be explicitly identified.

Brazelton et al. (1979) emphasize that competency in being involved in infants' early efforts with the caretaker is what makes it possible to elicit a response in the intersubjective field. The infant's innate understanding of the affective code is the earliest developmental trigger for shame. This is associated with a sense of inefficacy.

Broucek (1982, 1991), stressed the importance of a perceived failure in infancy, a failure to initiate, maintain or extend a desired emotional engagement with a caretaker.

A disruption in the "flow" of affective exchange could be looked upon as the trigger for shame. This sudden disruption of affective flow would bring about what Kaufman (1985) called the rupture of the interpersonal bridge. This interpersonal bridge is established through good-enough affective attunement on the part of caretakers so that an affective dialogue can take place between infant and caregiver based on reciprocity and complementarity in affective exchange (sometimes called flow) that promotes the development of the sense of self. By sense of self, I mean a self-awareness of an immediate, pre-conceptual type; it is the basis of our most profound identification with our body, and it is what provides us with the experience of "indwelling" the experience of the "lived body" rather than the body as a part of the object world.

Emde (1983) refers to a sense of self as "the pre-representational self" which he sees forming around an affective core, which guarantees our continuity of experience despite developmental change.

Silvan Tomkins, (1963), an affect theorist writes that experiences of shame are preceded by affective states of interest-excitement or enjoyment-joy rather than by negative affect states. Yet our clinical experience informs us that the experience of shame is frequent and pervasive in those persons whose affective states are primarily negative.

Tompkins' writing on shame reflects, however, a great sensitivity and understanding of the intersubjective context in which it is apt to occur. He had put it sensitively in his 1963 magnum opus in these words:

> If I wish to touch you but you do not wish to be touched,
> I may feel ashamed.

If I wish to look at you but you do not wish me to, I may feel ashamed.

If I wish you to look at me but you do not, I may feel ashamed.

If I wish to look at you and, at the same time, wish that you look at me, I can be shamed.

If I wish to be close to you but you move away, I am ashamed …

Morrison (1994) has a similar view: "Shame is elicited by an inter-subjective disjunction resulting in a sense of rejected desire and rejected affectivity, failed intentionality, and inefficacy. This is the result of mis-attunement.

Schore (1994) tries to tie the earliest experiences of shame to Mahler's practicing sub-phase of separation-individuation (twelve to eighteen months). He notes the function of shame as an inhibitor of hyper-aroused states when a practicing toddler, in an expansive grandiose, hyper-stimulated state of arousal, reunites with the caregiver expecting shared excitement and affective attunement but experiences instead a mis-attunement.

Creating an integrative understanding of neurological development and psychoanalytic concepts is undoubtedly a challenging task. However, we need to be aware of the importance of shame and its connection with objective self-awareness (OSA).

OSA appears to be the result of the interplay of developmental maturation of the central nervous system and social contextual factors such as conflicting points of view and disjunctive affectivity.

Amsterdam (1972) in her study of mirror self-image reactions in infants and toddlers before age two, concluded that "every subject who showed recognition behavior also manifested either avoidance or self-consciousness or all three." Those reactions point to a shame experience. Many of the behaviors that Mahler, Pine, and Bergman (1975) described as characteristic of the individuating child during the rapprochement sub-phase of separation-individuation may reflect the shame and ontological insecurity associated with the acquisition of OSA.

OSA makes possible the formation of a self-image, and later, with increasing cognitive maturation, a self-concept. At this point, standards, rules and goals (SRGs) begin to become increasingly important. Lewis (1992) notes failure with respect to SRGs may bring affective disjunction interpersonally as well as difficulty in maintaining a favorable self-image. It may be helpful to think of the earliest self-representation as a representation of a relationship, a representation more affective than conceptual in nature. Once firmly installed in the unconscious, it may be very resistant to change. Shame is elicited by an inter-subjective disjunction resulting in a sense of rejected desire and rejected affectivity, failed intentionality, and inefficacy. This is the result of mis-attunement" describes shame as a profound and painful experience rooted in a disconnect from others and a feeling of personal failing.

Shame induction is prevalent globally. Parents, teachers, and peers deliberately induce shame in children by use of power, overt verbal expressions of disgust or contempt, sadistic "teasing," and various forms of ostracism such as "the silent treatment" and love withdrawal.

Lewis believes love withdrawal elicits global self-evaluation of failure. It is also the most painful form of severance of the interpersonal bridge.

Shame is heavily influenced by cultural context and linguistic convention. Shame is an intensely social phenomenon, more dependent on cultural context than most other affects or dynamics. (Singer as a cultural anthropologist discusses the role of shame in several cultures)

A few case vignettes will help us understand more clearly these theoretical aspects of shame.

Case 1: Ms. G

Ms. G, a sixty-three-year-old analysand, had suffered inhibition in her mental activities. As an infant and during most of her childhood, her mother had suffered chronic depression, and her father had alcoholism with episodic temper outbursts. While growing up, Ms. G felt her mother was emotionally frozen. She had to be a chatterbox to get her attention or be super compliant to win her love. She thought she had to be vigilant to secure possible eye contact from her preoccupied mother. She learned that her early sense of pseudo-maturity cost her normal childhood playfulness and pleasure. The former state was mixed with an overdeveloped sense of self-sufficiency. She grew up struggling with poverty and emotional deprivation.

In one of her recent Monday sessions, she recovered a memory from her early childhood.

I was loitering at a slew near the shoreline with my two friends. We were around six years old or so. We threw rocks along the highway. The teacher saw us and reprimanded me. I hurried and told the teacher the name of a boy in our class and told her he had done it. I knew I was lying. I went home and could not sleep. The next day, I went up and told the teacher that it was not the boy who did it and that it was me. The teacher praised me in front of the class by telling everyone that at first G lied but she now came forward and told the truth.

At this point, G's tone of voice changed to self-mockery. "I was not a truthful kid! I was there to save my own skin. It was me who was a little forceful and instigated the whole rock-throwing incident. I was supposed to get home right after school, but instead I was loitering along the shore. My mom would not have noticed anyway for I was not noticeable at home."

I said, "You worried that you would be exposed and have to bear the humiliation feeling, if the truth were found. You felt an urgent need to save yourself." She responded, "Yeah, I was feeling mortified at the thought of being embarrassed in front of my classmates. I was not thinking about the boy who I was getting in trouble. It was myself I had to save."

Here we see it is not guilt as the motivating factor for stepping forward to tell the truth. It is a shame mechanism that was operating. She was horrified anticipating the risk of her affectionate tie to her teacher, a woman who cared for G a great deal to make sure she had proper meals or clothes when she came to school. G was very fond of her teacher and had a conscious wish to have her as her mother. She then said, "It was not altruistic of me to go and confess. It was me I was saving in her eyes."

Case 1: Jack

Jack is a nine-year-old white American boy who came to see me for treatment after his pediatrician referred him on March 1, 2005, because he would kick and hit his classmates. School authorities were very unhappy with his behavior and contemplated dismissing him. He was already expelled from two other schools for similar behavior. He was disruptive and ganged up with other boys to hit girls during recess time. He would bully older students when he was in kindergarten. He also hit his only friend on the swing set. He had superior intelligence and was in a GATE program.

There was a history of maternal mis-attunement and the birth of his younger brother when he was only 18 months was a major developmental trauma.

Two years into his analysis, when his aggressive symptoms disappeared and we worked through many important themes of his intra-psychic conflicts, he told me he was one of three students in his class picked for the spelling bee contest. He was in tears at the thought of the next step that required him to stand in front of the whole student body and participate in the contest. He became preoccupied with the terror of being gazed at and could not sleep the night before the big day. He also had the return of his original symptom of aggression.

He was mortified at the thought of not being able to spell words correctly in front of the whole student body. He was able to verbalize his wish not to be humiliated for guessing incorrectly. His primary narcissistic defenses were not going to be sufficient to save him from an anticipatory massive, disastrous failure. He imagined he was going to die in front of everyone, should he misspell a word. His anticipated failure to be a spelling bee star in relation to a failure to attain an ideal phallic power made him feel ashamed and mortified.

Case 2: Miss B

Miss B, a thirty-two-year-old unmarried Iranian woman, came to see me because of symptoms of depression, not knowing how to adjust to her new host country, the United States with its strange culture and social values. She came here to study at a major university in 1992 and lived on the East Coast with a friend of the family who offered to help her get started. After several years of living on the East Coast, she moved to the San Francisco Bay area. She wanted to be able to form a love relationship as well as work in her field of professional education and expertise. In one of her sessions, she recalled how in her home country, she felt oppressed, having to go to her classes wearing a head scarf and sitting in class with a partition between male and female students. She was experiencing feelings of rage and shame about how the female Islamic government official wiped her face with a piece of white cloth to see if there were any remains of makeup or lipstick. She felt ashamed and intruded upon by this forceful touch and the rubbing of her skin by a stranger.

The effect of the aroused, intense feelings of shame mixed with rage was quite palpable in the consulting room as she was narrating her experience. Her voice also changed as she recounted her memory of being treated indignantly. I said she must have felt humiliated and made to feel shame for a cause in which she had no faith. She was relieved that I understood her feelings, even though she appeared to be doubtful if I understood her fully. She said, "I was thinking how anyone could understand me if they had not experienced daily life in the political climate of the country I lived in as a youngster." She suspected I had come to the States long before the revolution. She went on to tell me that she was happy to leave Tehran behind, for she felt imprisoned and claustrophobic. To this day, when she sees some newly arrived immigrants who are still wearing headscarves, she has a very strong emotional reaction of embarrassment and shame, followed by feelings of anger. She wonders why they would not give up the scarf that is a symbol of their subjugation in the Islamic Republic now that they live in a free world.

We know the experience of shame from time to time about one's body is also part of normal development, especially during adolescence.

My patient in her late adolescence was forced to feel an intense body shame during that period of her life in her motherland. The memories of her body shame contributed to her self-consciousness to this day. She still has doubts about her appearance even though she is an attractive woman.

A third case illustrates how shame can be associated with cultural context and feeling fearful of being different.

Case 3: Mehran

Mehran was a first grader, a handsome boy of six from Afghanistan who entered treatment because of ritualistic behavior of hand washing. He was apprehensive about participating in play activities with other children in his school for fear of being treated badly since his skin color was just a shade or two darker. He worried about being criticized for imperfection by his teachers. He struggled to be successful. Mehran also showed unwillingness to work on tasks in the classroom and especially after school. He reported to his parents that he had "bad thoughts" when he started in analysis with me and kept repeating: "Oh, never mind"; "I don't remember my bad thought to tell you today!"; or "I don't want to say what I think out loud."

Mehran's underlying low self-esteem became obvious to his parents and to himself as well. Parental expectations of him to have scholastic success left more pressure on him to perform accordingly. He was not sure about his ability to make friends. He wished he would be accepted into the popular clicks and he could share the way he practiced the Moslem religion with his classmates. He wanted his friends to learn his ethno-cultural values too and accept him in their clique.

His mother infantilized him and treated him differentially like a little prince. She would also expect his two older sisters to do the same despite their expressed feelings of envy of their brother who was free to do what he pleased. His sisters resented the restricted freedom they had the way in which they dressed and in which their parents forbade them to talk to boys in their schools.

Mehran's relationship with his father contained many positive elements, but during his phallic and oedipal phase, his father showed concern about his obsessive-compulsive symptoms since he himself recalled being the same way as a young boy. His father wanted to pass his religious legacy to Mehran just like his father did by taking him to the holy city of Mecca. When he returned, he told me all about his trip and also recounted his adventure to his friends at school. His friends told him, "You are not supposed to talk about all of these weird things." He was ashamed and felt hurt. He did not know why they weren't interested in his travel story and why they were making fun of him. He came to one of his sessions in tears one day, telling me how enraged he was feeling. He wanted to do something "bad to them or at least tell them off" but could not. He was just mortified and felt frozen. He could not get any word out. I said he wanted to feel like one of them. Perhaps he felt they were seeing him being different and he wanted so badly to be accepted as who he was. After all, he liked to hear about their Sunday school church activities, and he wondered why was it they could not hear his story. He nodded his head in agreement and said, "We all go to the same school! Isn't that important?"

For him being in school with other boys connoted a strong denominator for belonging to the same crowd.

Here we see an example of a young boy who went through the affect of shame because of his social context that did not offer any understanding but labeled him as "strange and different."

Mehran failed to feel good about himself in relation to self-evaluation and standards for his lovability and acceptance among his peers in his school. He felt an imminent danger of social collapse from his rejection, and relegation to an inferior status, and loss of respect and ridicule by his peer group. The two cases of Jack and Mehran are different in their dynamic structure. Mehran's sense of shame is not based on the failure of ideal self, the representation of the goal of perfection in the subjective experience of the self, but failure of the school environment

His father decided he should go to a small private school after this incident, hoping he would be more accepted there.

The fourth case demonstrates the role parents play in the development of shame in their children.

Case 4: Mr. A

Mr. A, a thirty-three-year-old graduate student, came to analysis because of a myriad of symptoms. He was chronically depressed, and his life was constricted to the point that he was unable to make any decisions, even small ones. He had trouble staying in love relationships.

At age 17, he came to the United States to attend school and lived with a family friend for the first year. He continued his studies in his field but considered it to be his father's choice of career. He really wanted to do some other type of graduate work. Mr. A knew he was feeling rebellious toward his father whenever he would come to visit him. His mother was depressed, and his memories of her were of "a sad woman who was in bed a lot of time."

He felt helpless and ashamed of himself that he could not rescue his mother and could not stand up against his father's authority and tyranny. His father was overly critical and seemed to get angry much of the time.

Mr. A In one of his sessions, reported he was having difficulty getting along with his boss, a man he perceived as being judgmental and critical of him. He decided to voice his feelings to this man and let him know how he was making him feel. His assertion turned into an angry confrontation and made matters worse. It took Mr. A some time before he realized he acted out his feeling of father transference toward his boss.

In another session, he remembered how he was feeling helpless around his father and could not say anything to him or voice his opinion.

Mr. A remembered he liked reading poetry, but his father would criticizes him for being "too feeling, not enough of a man," especially when he found out his favorite poet was the contemporary Persian woman poet Forough Farrokhzad (2004). He liked her because she strived for personal freedom and individuality. He believed she accomplished much for Persian women through her life and her poetry. He wished his mother would have been strong and would have fought for her personal freedom as well.

In one of his analytic sessions, as he was remembering his childhood home, he fell into silence. When I inquired about him being silent, he said he was just remembering one of the Forough's poems, "the abandoned house." He felt the life that he left behind in Iran seemed very much like the poet's description of her life left behind.

When I inquired about his liking of her poetry and the meaning of the poem in those moments, he fell silent, he switched into his mother tongue and recited this poem, translated into English by me below.

I know now that from that distant home
Life's happiness has flown away.
I know now that a child in tears
Grieves over separation from his mother.

But I, upset and weary of spirit,
Head toward desire's road.
My lover is poetry, my solace is poetry.
I am going to seek my lover.

The poet imagined a sad, sleeping child in the arms of a tired, old nursemaid. And where "the candle in its own last flicker / sets out toward nothingness," she concluded with recognition of the real situation and her reason for abandoning her home.

Mr. A had identified with Forough's leaving her home just as he did in coming to the United States. He thought he would be accused of being "ungrateful" as his father told him on many occasions. Here in the United States his life was in his own hands and he felt free like the woman poet expressed in her poem. He feared that I would also find his liking of Forough rather odd as his father did. His father would say in a mocking tone that he was being a "sissy" knowing that he could have shown more interest in so many well-known male poets in Persian history. There's no scarcity of male poets after all!!

His father's words made him feel shame and he was feeling the re-emergence of his old feelings with me as well. Liking a woman poet instead of a man was perceived as a sign of not being like "a man" as his father wished him to be. He had to hide his interest from his father. He felt relieved that I was not judging him, and he even thought I might also like the poet.

Conclusion

These cases and the psychoanalytic theory illustrate some important developmental aspects of shame. Let me conclude with some general observations.

Shame is ubiquitous, a universal phenomenon. We can trace shame from the birth of human existence. Shame has been considered in philosophy, cultural anthropology, theology, and fiction. It permeates the Old Testament, although it tends to be replaced by guilt in the New. Other religions have also been influenced by shame.

Cultural anthropologists have noted distinctions between "shame" and "guilt" cultures. Although we have seen the absence of a focus on shame in psychoanalytical work, in recent years we have begun to reconsider its importance.

In dealing with our patients' shame, we inevitably ought to confront our own shame. There can be no awareness of a patient's experience of shame and humiliation without recognition of similar feelings and memories in oneself. The patient's shame jogs therapists' memories and reminds them of their own shame experience. This leads to hiding and concealing; it cloaks the patient's experience and results in a collusive ignoring of shame. Because of this collusion, I think shame has often remained unanalyzed. Recognition of the tendency to collude in ignoring shame should help therapists deal with this crucial affect.

In summary, first we need to keep in mind that people who undergo repeated shame experiences are more likely to have a substitute affect as rage or depression to disavow their feelings of shame.

As clinicians are becoming more observant of shame experiences in children, we recognize how difficult it may be for adult patients to access the feelings of shame and the memories that go with them. We need to make an active effort to open the feelings of shame to further analytic exploration.

Second, shame includes an affect, a searing painful affect. Vision is bound up with shame feelings. Shame about aspects of one's character or body image is experienced as subjective self-awareness.

For some, it is experienced as a fear or anticipatory dread of the scornful gaze of another person, similar to objective self-awareness.

Third, shame can generate defenses. The counterpart of shame may turn into shamelessness or extreme modesty as another defense.

Fourth, shame as an anticipatory affect can lead to anticipatory rejection, disgrace, ostracism, and relegation to inferior status—the impending social disaster called mortification.

Finally, Shame can also be a powerful and positive motivator for human interaction and engagement.

Much clinical research is needed to understand the phenomenon of shame. I hope my remarks have given you some ideas for future investigation into this topic of shame.

CHAPTER 7

Aggression and its management

How do we deal with aggressive behavior in children and adolescents? Does aggression in children turn into violence if not treated? How do we deal with therapeutic frame violation? What are the origins of these aggressive behaviors? How does the environment precipitate and encourage aggression? What is the role of media violent programming in aggression? How do socio-political factors influence these problems?

These important questions are beyond the scope of this chapter's discussion. Instead, I will present four cases and various intervention techniques in the therapeutic setting. Before my description of cases, I want to review some theoretical considerations about the origin of aggression in children.

We know that anger is a basic human emotion. It can be used adaptively in resolving conflict. It can be the cause of intense inner conflict, pain, and suffering. It can be used to manipulate others, and it can lead to aggressive, destructive, and violent behavior toward others. Freud (1930, 1933a) was right that violence is a part of the human condition. We see an increasing number of young children perpetrate violent crimes, sometimes in places we thought were safe—our schools or homes. We wonder why children resort to violent behavior when they feel angry or slighted. What had gone wrong?

Is violence among children connected to a chaotic environment, neglect, abandonment, and abuse in infancy and early childhood? Bowlby (1994) connected violence with abandonment. The absence of emotional ties to love objects is thought of as a cause for predatory violence. Greenacre (1941) thought anxiety was the root of violence. She wondered if severe trauma, pathological parent–child interactions, sexual over-stimulation, or unrelieved organismic distress during the first three years of life would compromise self-regulatory functions; and neuro-physiological patterning might be affected. The child is left as a vulnerable, easily overwhelmed individual.

Greenacre's ideas are substantiated by psychoanalytic observation, attachment research, and recent work in neuroscience. Stressful, unpredictable, and violent home environments, disorganized attachment, and early trauma compromise emotional regulatory systems. Early intervention and possible treatment models can help these children.

Contemporary research substantiates many of these early hypotheses. Attachment disorder and pathological parent–child interactions, unpredictable environments, neglect, abuse, and out-of-home placement (as in unfriendly and hostile foster parent homes) are correlated with excessive anger and violent behavior.

Twemlow, Fonagy & Sacco (2005) have outlined a health policy attitude for a project that intervenes in multi-problem families. The proposal encourages mentalization and reduces coercive power dynamics. Such families who are considered socially high risk often have multiple problems with school communities as well as social services and the criminal justice system. These are families who have several generations of individuals with borderline personality disorders, substance abuse, post-traumatic stress disorders, exposure to violence and lack of family support.

A broad range of psychopathology has been seen as one or another form of specific mentalizing dysfunction. The mind is misperceiving or misinterpreting the status of its own contents and its own functions. PTSD may entail a collapse of mentalizing, and therapy aims at the restoration of normal mentalization.

I believe the concepts of agency, self-regulation (including affect regulation), and mentalization are important. We need to describe these concepts before suggesting some ideas for intervention in the treatment situation. Providing developmental models of affect regulation can be an important therapeutic intervention. The importance of timely intervention in early childhood aggressive disturbance ought to be emphasized in daycare centers and the home environment. I will present several cases and describe treatment models and strategies that help these children develop a greater capacity for affective modulation and tolerance.

Aaron

Aaron, age four and a half, is angry and upset that his foster mother does not give him his favorite stuffed animal to take with him every day to the early child center. He throws temper tantrums and hits and bites other children at the center. His foster mother thinks he is very demanding, and she gets infuriated with him. Although he was in several foster homes, his most recent foster mother, Mrs. M, took a liking to him; and has been thinking seriously about adopting him, but gets doubtful about adoption when Aaron acts out or demands that his bedroom has to remain unchanged and objects have to be in the same spot as he left them. For example, if juice spills on his shirt, he demands to have a new shirt or a new pair of shoes if his old ones get dirty. He becomes easily angered and will scream and bite. Mrs. M's tolerance was running short, and she worried she might lose her temper and hurt him physically. Thus, she was referred to me for parent guidance treatment.

George

At age twelve, George was expelled from yet another in a series of schools because his teachers could not manage his angry outbursts and abusive behavior toward his classmates. His father would punish him whenever he disobeyed or wanted to get his own way and His mother would also over-interpret his intentions during those incidents and become fearful for her own life and his stepfather challenged him once when he said he was not going to clean up after himself by saying in a testing tone of voice "Let's see what you will do when I make you do it!" George lost his temper and then threw a glass full of orange juice he took from the counter at his stepfather. His mother then called the police who considered him a danger to others and admitted him to the hospital for further evaluation. During the course of the treatment, it became apparent that his mother, who had a history of being abused physically and sexually by her father, and would thus regard any normal behavior as aggressive. She therefore expected that her son would also get out of control and hurt his family members or cause other damage.

John

John, age four and a half, was referred by his pediatrician to me because he was violent to his classmates in kindergarten and attacked his only friend from behind on a swing set. His mother was unable to control his angry attacks on her and his younger brother who was one- and one-half years his junior. She would often behave at his age level and get into a physical fight with him as though she were his sibling, then be remorseful. She was afraid of losing her control and hurting John. He would make farting (by putting his hand under his armpit or under his knee), shrieking, or animal noises in the class and say mean words to his teachers and classmates.

In my psychoanalytic work with John and parental work with his mother, I was able to establish a dialogue in which experiences, thoughts, and emotions could be labeled and integrated. During the first several sessions, he would come and crawl on the floor in the waiting room, making animal sounds and refuse to come into the consultation room. I observed this behavior several times and paid attention to his mother, noticing she was overwhelmed and desperately needed my help. At the same time, she communicated to me, "See how impossible he is! It can't be my fault if he is this way." I commented to him, "It made you feel stronger and better sounding this way, especially when you feel that you could not show your big, angry, fighting feelings. You wish it were not so hard for you to become the boss of your feelings." After one or two promptings on my part, he abruptly stopped the animal sounds and sat on the. I said, "We would do better if you and I could play together inside the playroom and try to figure out a way to make you to become the boss of your big feelings."

I told him, "You expect bad things could happen when you get mad at your mother; and also, not knowing what I would do or feel if you get mad at me." He accepted my request to come inside the room. He was interested in exploring the board games and the toys. During his playtime, I was able to respond to his affective tone and dysregulation and our interactions continued to move in a more trusting, positive direction and timely responsive manner.

He learned that I would take his feelings very seriously and respond empathetically to his distress, particularly when he had a bad day at school or a tough time with his mother. Our interaction over some period of time helped him feel safe and he was able gradually to name and contain his feelings and be less frightened by them. This process helped gradually a new shift in his self-containment and self-organization.

Some of the time through storytelling and narrative work, I helped him imagine how his feelings could be understood and labeled. I was able to label his feelings and actions in order to move and lift his behavioral problems to a level of mental representation and symbolization. He could then label his own feelings and action in order to move his behavioral problems to levels of mental representation and symbolization, and he learned how emotions could be modulated and mastered. After one year of intensive therapy, he was able to use metaphors to elaborate emotional states through symbolic play. I have continued working with him as well as seeing his mother in weekly parent work to help her master her feelings when she becomes overwhelmed.

Anna

Anna at age seven was brought to see me because her teachers were at a loss about how to deal with her aggressive behavior, for she was hitting her classmates and stealing food from their lunch boxes. Her mother also had a difficult time managing her at home. Her younger brother was born when she was seventeen months old, and her younger sister when she was five.

She wished that her brother would just drop dead, and she would be the happiest child in her school.

Her family immigrated to the States when Anna was two years old. Her mother had a difficult time acculturating to the new environment. She was very critical of other mothers, and she felt inferior to them since they seemed to be more interested in the lives of their children. Anna was more of her pal than a daughter, who was confused about her mother's inconsistent rules at home.

Her play was disorganized and chaotic, involving destruction and murdering family dolls with sadistic pleasure.

I helped Anna mourn the loss of her country of origin in order to become available to Anna's deprived inner world.

She suffered from a deficient sense of agency and insecure attachment. The generational boundary between mother and daughter was blurred, and the rules and regulations at home were disregarded since there was confusion about parental authority. Her treatment involved my active parent work, especially with her mother, and analytical play therapy work with Anna. Helping the parental superego to make Anna recognize herself as an active agent was part of my treatment strategy. Anna had to learn to differentiate between desire, emotion and the consequence of impulsive actions.

A sense of agency

The importance of partial presence or total absence of the sense of agency in self-regulation is quite evident in the above cases.

William James (1890) first described the "sense of agency." There are two components, "me" and "I." The "me" part was given considerable attention in psychoanalysis, and the "I" part which refers to the self-concept is one's sense of self as an active agent. The I self is the intentional designer, creator, instigator, organizer, actor, regulator and manager of all activity. The I self is the chief executive who brings about action; the instrument of that action and the self-action is what brings about change.

Fonagy and his colleagues write that a sense of agency requires a sense of the self as an intentional mental being. Actions are deliberate. Children come to realize that there are links between actions and feelings; the idea that agency must include a sense of the self as an intentional mental being builds on the work of Fonagy (2001) with his colleagues. He defines mentalization or "reflective function," as a capacity to form and reflect on representations of mental states that is thoughts and feelings:

1.   Becoming aware that thoughts and feelings are lodged internally in the mind.
2.   Thinking about and reflecting on them.
3.   Realizing that others also have thoughts and feelings.

Mentalization also involves perceiving that not only one's own behavior but also the behavior of others can be understood in terms of thoughts and feelings, beliefs and desires—that is, mental states.

Understanding the feelings of others helps us to make sense of and to anticipate their actions. Once children recognize that they can have intentions or desires without acting on them, they are faced with the challenge of self-responsibility. In recognizing the "I" self as the master, the agent, the chief executive of all thoughts, feelings, desires and actions, this "I" self becomes accountable for those thoughts, feelings, desires and actions.

Self-responsibility involves accountability for one's actions, but also for one's feelings, impulses, motives, and desires. It involves "owning up to one's needs and impulses as one's own" (Loewald, 1979, p. 392). This means acknowledging ownership of one's angry, hateful, envious, jealous, competitive, vengeful, destructive, greedy, and murderous feelings, admitting guilt, and not blaming others for their existence.

This is a developmental challenge for any child, and we know there is a lag between the child's recognition of the feelings that follow actions, perceiving fault and admitting guilt (Anna Freud, 1936, p. 119). Yet a mature sense of agency requires this kind of self-responsibility. Self- responsibility also involves mastery. Angry feelings in their many forms are ubiquitous; they come with the human condition.

Related conflicts, whether interpersonal or intra-psychic, at whatever developmental level never become fully "resolved." This is because the emotional challenges that arouse these feelings are also part of the human condition. The developmental challenge influences the creation of a sense of mastery. It is taking ownership of them, and then finding the most adaptive way of gaining control over these feelings, desires, and impulses rather than feelings and desires being in control. Anna Freud once said that the task for the child in early childhood is to learn to be in control of the drives instead of the drives being in control of the child. In fact, it is the task of every human being regardless of age to learn to be in control of one's emotions.

A competent sense of self also needs a sense of organization, cohesion and stability over time. Self-regulation requires the capacity for self-reflection, mastery over feelings, desires and impulses, as well as flexible response. Owning and developing mastery over one's feelings, desires, and impulses requires some competence in keeping these feelings, desires and impulses within manageable limits.

By keeping them within manageable limits, the feelings do not disorganize and overwhelm self-regulatory functions. Self-regulation relies on the capacity to utilize the signaling function of affect:

First, the child must be able to identify, label and reflect on feelings as they begin to emerge.

Second, the child must also have sufficient frustration tolerance to be able to delay automatic reflexive response, and instead, exercise control over emotional response systems.

Third, through the process of imitation, introjections and identification with the caregiver, the maturation of affective regulation becomes solidified.

The self-regulatory agent would have to attend to all aspects of the current situation, retrieve conscious and unconscious memories of similar past situations. This involves being able to fantasize about the possible consequences of one action versus another. The ability to reflect on possible associated affective states and integrate all of this relevant information in the mind, review and compare a number of possible plans, and decide which actions and emotional procedures would be most effective and adaptive.

Finally, the mind would be able to execute an effective decision. This entire process takes place unconsciously and almost instantaneously. But the ability to process affects in this way equips the mind to avoid the disorganization and distress that results from intense and overwhelming emotional arousal.

The self can be experienced as a regulating agent. Developing a capacity to self-regulate requires the caregiver to provide structure, consistency, and safety, involving consistent rules, regulations, and parental expectations. The child has to develop a capacity to tolerate frustration and adhere to the rules of society. Rules at home and school and in society are in conflict with the child's desire. As a result, feelings of intense anger, hate, protest and rage may erupt. Safety and predictability during such times of conflict are essential.

For caregivers, providing structure and consistency can be a challenge if they suffer from fragile psychic structures and consequently more vulnerable to their own affective storms. The caregiver must resist being drawn into the child's normal angry protests to rules and restrictions and should withstand provocation. The caregivers' role is to maintain safety and distinguish between their own emotions and those of the child. This allows them to be empathic to the feelings and needs of the child while providing a regulating balance to intervene before the child becomes overwhelmed. The caregiver must absorb the child's ambivalence and rage, contain and label the feelings, and at the same time remain firm and consistent with the child's demands and expectations.

If caregivers or therapists can "survive" the child's projection (Winnicott, 1969), they can help the child progressively differentiate the inner world of psychic reality and emotional reaction from the outside world of real experience. Symbolic play can be particularly helpful at this time. Play is an important means by which a child repeats and masters traumatic experiences, which was one of Freud's early observations in child development (1920g, p. 14).

The research of Fonagy and his colleagues (2002, p. 257) indicates that children of three or four generally make little distinction between the inner world of psychic reality and the outer world of real experience. Although cognitively they distinguish the two, they live in the inner world of emotions; their perceptions and the meanings they assign to them are not felt to be representations, but rather direct replicas of reality. Consequently, it feels true to them.

However young children also use a pretend mode. In their pretend mode, ideas, wishes, and fantasies are representational. The idea and what it symbolizes can be distinguished and manipulated. Symbolizing, labeling and verbalizing thoughts and emotions through pretend play enables the child to elaborate the inner world of wishes, fears, feelings, and fantasies, and gain some control and mastery over their feelings (Katan, 1961).

If the therapist can create what Winnicott called a play space, the therapist can become a part of this process and help the child distinguish his inner world of angry feelings which lead to angry projections and views of the mother or caregiver as a frightening and punishing figure from the mother of real experience. The child can then use the therapist to reflect on the feelings, and find flexible and adaptive ways of expressing and managing rage and other distressing feelings. Thus, finding adaptive and flexible ways of compromise and conflict resolution helps the child to contain his or her feelings. In doing so, the child learns that intense affects such as anger and rage can be managed and regulated.

Rewards in the form of recognition and praise for their efforts as well as for success are essential to the child's developing capacity to tolerate frustration and capability to adhere to rules and expectations. The satisfaction and pride shared between the mother–child dyad can be fostered by following rules and parental guidance. Such sharing of positive emotions generates a sense of pride. It also fosters the development of moral emotions as the caregiver's rules and moral values gradually become those of the child through the process of "internalization." Not only are these self-regulatory functions supported and enhanced by the structure, consistency and safety provided by the caregiver; but this also helps the child become increasingly aware of the links between intentions, actions, consequences, and emotional states.

Ideally the child gradually begins to associate following the rules with shared pleasure. In addition there is a realization that bereft and lonely feelings follow bouts of hateful rage or refusal to comply. Once a child recognizes choices between desires and actions, anticipates consequences and responds to anger and anxiety with verbalization instead of action or repression, we as clinicians see important evidence that the child is beginning to use the signal function of affects. Using affects as signals of danger enables the child to become increasingly competent in emotional regulation and a more effective self-agent.

Perry et al. (1997) has found that young children who grow up within an environment of chronic stress, disturbed attachment and lack of the reciprocal verbal dialogues that foster effective skills often develop excessively active and reactive stress response apparatuses. These children are unable to integrate their own mental states and consequently become hyper-vigilant to environmental cues, particularly non-verbal ones, and hypersensitive to physiological anxiety. They then develop maladaptive emotional procedures that predispose them to peremptory reflexive responses such as rage, anxiety and fear.

Conclusion

The children I presented have a disorganized, impoverished sense of self and inadequate sense of agency. They have not experienced sensitive mirroring, safety or comfort, nor have they experienced an intersubjective dialogue with their caregivers. Therefore, the basic tools for thinking, labeling and reflecting on their emotions and intentions are missing. Although they may recognize themselves as the active agents of certain physical actions, they do not appear to understand the concept of choice, that their actions are intentional and deliberate, and that not all impulses and desires need to be acted upon. That is, they do not recognize themselves as intentional mental beings.

Unable to recognize their actions as deliberate results of their intentions and choices, they are unable to reflect on their actions and recognize links between their actions, consequences, and subsequent painful affective states. They are unable to take responsibility for their actions. Instead, their actions are reflexive and are experienced as reactive impulses to environmental provocations.

These children also have little capacity for delay, self-control, and self-regulation. Their inner world is a chaotic one. They lack the capacity to label and think about their emotions and recognize links between their actions, consequences, and feelings. They have little executive control over emotional response systems and lack the higher order of integrative processes that make self-reflection, self-regulation and flexible response possible. Their marked insecurity and narcissistic vulnerability lead them to focus their attention on controlling others. They are not able to regulate their affects, fear and panic. Consequently, they end up with disrupted self-regulation.

Psychoanalytic intervention with very young children due to their innate brain plasticity and the resiliency in their psychological functioning presents a hopeful prospect for child analysts. The new direction in our work with such children ought to take into consideration two important principles. These important principles in the treatment of such cases involve fostering a sense of safety and secure attachment, and a timely response to a child's distress, helping to create an optimal play space. Therefore, it is of utmost importance to set limits and provide a consistently predictable structure for the child. A parent–child dialogue is also necessary for the child to develop a capacity to use affects as signals.

PART III

SELFHOOD

CHAPTER 8

Ethnic identity formation[5]

Immigration is a complex biopsychosocial process with the capacity to mobilize the destabilization of the psychic structure, which can profoundly influence identity formation (Akhtar, 1994, 1999). Destabilization is a gradual process, and resiliency will be required to restructure the ego and reestablish an optimal psychic equilibrium.

The immigration experience affects identity development throughout the life cycle (Akhtar, 2004), especially during the separation-individuation phases of infancy, adolescence, and adulthood. Immigrant mothers, in particular, carry the shadow of their former lives within their newly found identities in their host countries (Mann, 2004). The nature of a mother's past life in her homeland, combined with the slow but steady change in identity as an immigrant, creates a complexity of experience that involves language acquisition, polyglotism[6], and other cultural variants—factors that significantly influence identity formation among all immigrants, but particularly among immigrant mothers. These influences, in turn, affect the separation-individuation processes of their children in the new country. The immigrant mother's secure

---

5 Originally published as Mann, M. (2006). The formation and development of individual and ethnic identity: Insights from psychiatry and psychoanalytic theory. *The American Journal of Psychoanalysis, 66*(3): 211–224. https://doi.org/10.1007/s11231-006-9018-2. Reproduced with permission.

6 Amati-Mahler (1995) describes polylinguism as acquisition of various languages in childhood. Polyglotism is learning a language later in life, based on translation.

base is lost, and if the cultural assimilation becomes complete, a newly found secure base is reborn and reconstructed.

On an internal level, the immigrant mother fluctuates between extremes of distance from her native self-representation and her newly emerging self-representation as a resident of the adopted country. The struggle in self-identity formation becomes a complex process since the immigrant mother must negotiate her own physical and psychological separation from her infantile object to stabilize her adult experience of parenthood and adapt to a new culture and language. This, in turn, influences her changing conceptualization of self and other in her individuation process.

Failure to successfully negotiate the distance between these self-representations can result in two problematic outcomes of identity (Teja & Akhtar, 1981): ethnocentric withdrawal and counter-phobic assimilation. As Winnicott (1965) described, "false" and "true" selves, alternating phases of closeness and distance from one or the other culture, may intensify the splitting of the self and the object world.

Unlike mature adults, adolescents do not have the inner stability to support appropriate levels of impulse control, because they are in the process of integrating their standard of conduct. Adolescents normally look to parents to prevent them from letting their impulses get out of control. They look to their parents to keep their impulses from overwhelming them.

The immigrant mother struggling with her own sense of identity formation is not emotionally available to help her adolescent children with the assistance they need to deal with and be able to create a sense of mastery over their anxiety.

Adolescence is a massive upheaval, characterized by fluctuations between regression and progression, dependency and self-reliance, gender issues related to being male or female, passivity and activity, as well as control and submission. The organizations of the ego, id, and superego lessen, and when this is accompanied by changes in immigration to a new host country, it could potentially create sets of new outcomes for the adolescent (Mehta, 1998).

The immigrant mother, on the other hand, shaped by the influences of her child's transformation into adolescence, loss of power at home, as well as in her new social world outside her family life, faces a sense of incompetency on many levels, especially the acquisition and use of a new language. A lack of competency in the newly acquired language, and fear of having to replace their culture of origin with an unfamiliar new culture bring about mourning for the loss of her symbolic, original mother tongue. Thus, her adult individuation process becomes affected or even delayed. This can lead to an intense awareness of her loss of parental authority. This mandates the enlisting of defenses and coping mechanisms, in order to help her adapt to the two co-existing, contradicting and contrasting worlds of languages, customs, mores and landscapes. Having to give up part of one's sense of individuality creates intra-psychic tension, which taxes the mother's ego structure.

Language

The immigrant's native language is the most trustworthy link to the maternal attachment figure and the culture in which she was nourished and raised. The mother tongue is a link to the earliest maternal imago. The new language may not be valued and is possibly marred with ambivalent feelings depending on the circumstances of migration. If migration is forced, as in the case of an exile, the ambivalent conflict may be more prominently expressed.

The immigrant moves in and out of two linguistic worlds; an obliged distancing from the mother tongue and in a parallel way, an obliged entry into a foreign land of new and unfamiliar-sounding words. Constant navigation between these two worlds adds to the splitting of self-representation. The fear of losing one's familiar linguistic world and the fear of not being able to take ownership of the newly acquired language because of one's ambivalent feelings make the reconciliation of these two worlds more challenging.

Adopting a new language in a new land can present a threat to self-identity and can disrupt the inner maternal representation of the mother tongue. Inner maternal conflict regarding language acquisition in the new country brings about a loyalty conflict both in mothers and their adolescent children, which in turn, impacts their relationship. If the immigrant mother perceives the new language as a threat to her maternal bonding with her adolescent child, she might unconsciously reject it or make a hostile attack to lacerate the new language. She might feel as if she is being replaced by a new imaginary stepmother for her child.

Constantly being spoken to in a language other than one's mother tongue can be burdensome to the immigrant mother, especially when there is a lack of emotional refueling.

Some adolescent children, who do understand their mother's native tongue, yet cannot converse in that language, respond in English. This may widen the gap in the mother–child dyad. The resolution of splitting the self and the object world requires a robust affect regulation, a good-enough capacity for mentalization, a holding on to social affiliation, and a reasonable passage of time for healing.

Self-identity and cultural identity

The strength of an immigrant mother's self-identity and cultural identity before migration has a great impact on her resiliency and capacity for adaptation to the new culture. Mothers with an unstable pre-immigration personality structure are at greater risk of transgressing and regressing into identity dissolution in the face of life's challenges. They have more difficulty tolerating their loneliness in the new land without extended family and social support.

Furthermore, mothers who themselves have not achieved the psychic capacity for their mid-life separation-individuation process have greater difficulty when their adolescents reach their own need to emancipate psychologically. The transformation of children into adolescents and young adults, and their separation-individuation processes impact their mother's individuation. Through a mourning process, the mother would let go of youthful aspects of the self and replace them with the realization that a mid-life self can bring about greater autonomy and competency.

The term separation-individuation by Blos (1967) refers to adolescent transition, moving from close ties to the parent to the newly, more autonomous self. It has also been applied to the physical migration. The adolescent may attempt to disengage from his or her mother due to the threat of-merging with her. Thus, the adolescent alternates between approaching and moving away from the mother, as well as idealizing and devaluing her. This back and forth can pose a greater threat to the immigrant mother's intra-psychic separateness.

The new identity of an immigrant mother who does not have pre-immigration character-structure problems becomes consolidated into a reconstructed ego identity involving unconscious identification with the new culture. These newly borrowed identifications become integrated with the old, inherited culture of the country of origin.

The immigrant mother with a fragile, pre-existing, pre-immigration ego identity is prone to be fragmented, partial and multiple identities leading to identity diffusion. There seems to be elasticity in the emerging expression of hybrid identity in certain psychosocial settings, where one or the other self-identity appears to be prominent. Searles' (1986) view supports this notion that a healthy identity does not possess a monolithic solidity.

Loss and mourning

The maternal immigrant faces cultural shock, and numerous losses and mourns for what was left behind. She mourns the loss of familiar surroundings, the presence of loved ones, familiar food, customs, and, perhaps most importantly, the familiar cadence of her mother tongue. Feelings of guilt, anxiety, and fear are mixed with her mourning. The mourning process causes a serious disequilibrium in the individual's identity. The intra-psychic turmoil is a vestige of the second individuation process of adolescence (Blos, 1967). Survivor guilt over having left family members and fellow countrymen behind, the anxiety over the anticipated loss of her long-held value system, and the fear that she will be viewed as a misfit within the new culture, are dominant.

Once the mourning process moves toward liberation with the help of therapeutic intervention and social support, the mother becomes emotionally available to make a progressive move toward autonomy and identity consolidation. The mourning–liberation process of immigration results in a reconsolidated hybrid identity in individuals who are resilient and have good-enough adaptive self and object representations.

There are many questions one can ask: What does the new culture offer to immigrant mothers, and at what cost to their cultural identity? How do they adapt to the American cultural myth and individuality of the American character, so foreign to their own? It is of clinical interest to observe these mothers who navigate their identity dissolution and the building of a new cultural identity. Insulation and loneliness are inevitable outcomes when immigrant mothers strive to preserve the culture and language of their motherland in the new host country. These important issues lend themselves to other possible psychoanalytic technical dimensions relevant to our work as psychotherapists and psychoanalysts.

Sense of belonging

Immigration challenges one's sense of belonging in the host country. The sense of isolation and loneliness is interrelated with the sense of belonging. Living in the hope of someday returning to one's country of origin impedes the mourning process and the newcomer's assimilation into the foreign culture. The immigrant deals with his or her perspective of the past—alive in the present—without a clear boundary formation.

The clinician must be aware of the profound significance that linguistic differences play in the therapeutic and psychoanalytic setting. These differences play an important role in the psychological outcome of the analytical process with immigrant populations. Lack of sensitivity to them can cause mis-attunement, lack of understanding, or misunderstanding of cultural nuances in the therapeutic dyad, and can further traumatize immigrants.

The analyst, working with an immigrant population, also faces complex identity transformation issues in the therapeutic dyad. It means that in doing analytical work with immigrant populations, the analyst inevitably goes through a re-working of his or her identity structure. This has important counter-transference implications, which are beyond the scope of this chapter.

The case of Jason, an adolescent, indicates how the shadow of an immigrant mother's past maternal identity and her multiple cultural identities influence her son's self-identity formation. Different challenges arose during the various developmental stages in the case of an adolescent, Jason, whose mother's immigration issues had an impact on his psychic development.

Case of Jason, an Iraqi-American adolescent

The family doctor referred Jason, a seventeen-year-old adolescent, for treatment of depression and performance anxiety. In our first session, he said, "I feel I am smothered by my parents, especially my mother. When I am around them, I feel down, short-tempered, miserable, and terrible. My whole life should be focused on school only. That is what they expect of me."

Jason's parents initially contacted me through their family physician because they knew I was Persian and spoke Farsi, the language of their childhood. They also knew I could not speak Arabic, a language that they spoke as their mother tongue. They believed I would understand their cultural expectations and their Assyrian-Iraqi background far better than other doctors.

Background

Jason's grandparents on both sides of his family migrated from Iraq to Northern Iran as young couples. Both of Jason's parents were born in Iran and have been friends since childhood. In their initial evaluation sessions, they relayed fond memories of their motherland, and of their tears, confusion, and upset when they had to leave. At the age of eight, Jason's mother and her family suddenly were uprooted from their familiar surroundings. Without explanation, they moved to Iraq, where they continued to live for almost two decades. Jason's father's family-followed their friends' family to Iraq, where Jason's parents both earned degrees in architecture, and ultimately married each other. Their families were very supportive of their union since they had a long history together.

The young married couple decided to migrate a third time, this time to the United States. By this time, both were professionals in their twenties and left Iraq by choice, not out of political or economic necessity. They settled in Atlanta, Georgia, where Jason and his two younger sisters were born, and then moved to the Bay Area in northern California, their fourth migration. The landscape and climate of northern California reminded them of the coastal region around the Caspian Sea in Iran, the motherland of their early childhood.

Jason's mother tried hard to be a perfect mother—an unattainable ideal. She paid a good deal of attention to her children's physical health and social interaction with their peers. She was raised with the help of an extended family and good social support. However, she had to raise her children without any extended family, by herself, in a foreign country.

Jason had two younger sisters, ages twelve and eleven. The elder sister was born when Jason was four years old. In an early session, he recalled his mother coming home from the hospital with a bundle in her arms, his new sister. The following year, another baby sister was added to the family.

Early childhood

In his preschool years, Jason was afraid of the dark and anxious about his mother's safety. Upon entering kindergarten, he displayed separation anxiety and fear that his mother would forget to pick him up at the end of his school day, behavior his parents believed he would grow out of. His mother also had panic attacks over the thought of losing her children, particularly Jason to kidnappers.

Jason's IQ was tested at the beginning of kindergarten. Due to his superior intelligence, he was able to skip kindergarten and move directly into the first grade. In elementary school, he proved himself a good student, but his parents expected him to be excellent.

He was not allowed to have sleepovers or stay at a friend's house, and this turned into a major source of tension. On Halloween, Jason was not allowed to go trick or treating with his friends for fear of getting poisoned with candies. His mother's paranoia was at its height on this specific holiday.

Adolescent years

Jason was allowed to play clarinet in the school band and was on the basketball team. His family supported his athletic abilities by driving him for three hours each way to another city, so he could play on the team. Jason had a few good friends whose parents were also immigrants. His effort to make friends with Anglo children was faced with maternal disapproval. Jason had many clashes with his mother over familial rules and expectations. He wanted to be like other children. He did not want to be reminded by his mother that his ethnic background was superior to others. This notion was confusing for Jason who wanted to blend in with his friends, not stand out among them.

Historically, Jason had been a good student, but he failed several courses in his freshman year of high school. He was interested in girls but knew he had to hide his sexual attraction from his family, especially his mother who was not familiar with the concept of dating in this country. She grew up in a culture where dating was non-existent. Young girls and boys would go out as a group to social or sports events, but never would a young man or woman go out as a couple. Marriages were primarily arranged, and dating was a much more serious proposition with an implication that a marriage proposal would soon occur.

In high school, Jason's best friend invited him to sleep over at his house; once again his mother prevented him from doing so. She believed this would be culturally unacceptable. Jason began to rebel against his parents' authority and expressed his anger by neglecting his grades. It was at this juncture with his academic failure that his parents sought my help.

The initial therapeutic process

In our first session, Jason complained angrily about being smothered by his mother.

He reported that she monitored him closely and insisted that he should be an obedient son.

He told me that his father had finally accepted his son's interest in studying international relations since he did not want to follow his father's career path as an architect. This was an important message to me. Jason had his own separate interests and did not want to abide by his father's wishes. He felt angry with his parents for rejecting his desire to enroll in a summer program at a prestigious university out of state, insisting instead that he live at home and attend a nearby school for the summer.

After four months of twice-weekly psychotherapy and twice-monthly parent counseling sessions, I recommended four-times-weekly psychoanalysis for Jason. His parents' reaction was an enormous shock; they interpreted this recommendation as a sign of their parental failure. However, they were willing to give therapy a try, with the understanding that Jason and I had only one year to work together before he entered college.

Course of analytic treatment

Jason's analytical work with me began as a struggle around how he was being transported to my office by his mother for appointments. He found me helpful when he came twice weekly, but at four times a week, he began to see me as someone who was controlling his life, just like his mother. He became angry with me and threatened to stop coming to our sessions. At the same time, however, he was curious about my background and my life in the United States.

Transference

Jason engaged with me in an intense transference relationship that contained both oedipal and pre-oedipal levels of conflict, displaying both aggressive and sexual elements. The consistent interpretation of defense in the context of the supportive parental work I provided allowed him to be more mature in his use of less primitive defenses and to articulate his feelings with insight.

I knew Jason's analysis would be interrupted when he moved away to attend college, and that our time was limited. I reminded him that it mattered what opinion he expressed in our decision to continue our work together as we had done in the past. He had friends whom he felt were untroubled and high achievers. He was happy to excel in high school and hoped he would be admitted into a prestigious university upon graduation.

Jason raised many questions about his parents and wondered why they could not become more assimilated to American culture, as he imagined that I was. He knew his parents' migration history and noticed their visible comfort and relaxed demeanor when they spoke with someone of a similar linguistic and cultural background. On one occasion, Jason became furious that I was not sharing my life history; he felt it was not fair that he told me all about his life without knowing much about mine. When I suggested that we needed to figure out what was so upsetting to him, he immediately responded,

You know my mother shows her mixed feelings about having left her country and living here in the States, and I can tell that she is upset, having left her own country that she misses very much. You have not told me what was it like for you when you first arrived. You don't seem to have this trouble like my mom.

When I suggested that perhaps he was worried his mother's ambivalence would turn into his own ambivalence about coming to see me, Jason nodded. Furthermore, he worried that his mixed feelings would make the good trust we had built together go away, and that would make him upset and confused. Perhaps he felt unsure if I would be able to help him with his "scary, big angry feelings" toward his mother, and toward me.

Jason was unconsciously testing maternal object representation with his newly formed developmental object, the analyst. How well he could integrate both of these object representations in the face of maternal ambivalence was my question and remained to be seen. How Jason would discover his own individuality, and sense of self-identity with his natural talents and abilities, in order to better integrate his ego function, was another big question on my mind.

Role reversal and translator role

During my weekly parental work with the mother, I realized that she had many conflicted feelings. Her anxiety, guilt, and shame had roots in her cultural imperatives and her deeply held fear that her competency as a mother was sorely deficient in the context of her new environment. Her anxiety was embedded in her inability to communicate with her children in a distant and borrowed language.

She feared losing her status as their parental authority. She had to rely on her children, especially Jason, to translate in many social situations in which she could not comprehend what was being communicated. Furthermore, she was ambivalent about learning American English and eventually becoming a polyglot who could easily slip in and out of her triple language worlds.

The role reversal that can occur between teenagers and their parents is an important phenomenon in immigrant families, with root causes partly connected to language and custom acquisition. Jason had mixed feelings about being the translator in his family. He regularly faced situations where his mother was not able to make sense of what she heard while shopping, visiting her children's school, and in a host of other social situations. On the one hand, Jason felt burdened; yet, on the other hand, he felt elevated to a superior position of parental authority beyond his actual capability of being an adolescent. He felt more like a parent or a teacher, in comparison to his mother. This change in Jason's status occurred more frequently when he was with his mother, for his father played the traditional role of a reliable provider who spent most of his time at work with his fellow engineer coworkers and friends.

Immigrant mothers and identity formation

Among many interwoven themes that emerged during Jason's therapy, one in particular centered on his cultural and self-identity. This is only one part of our work that reflects his struggles pertaining to the role his mother played in his identity formation.

Since their arrival in the United States, Jason's parents have remained ethnocentric and devalued American culture as being too independent and "wild." They attributed much of Jason's behavior to the American way of life and criticized him for this. His desire to connect with his peer group, many of whom belonged to other cultural backgrounds, provoked parental disapproval. His parents' rules and expectations were inconsistent with those of Anglo-American teenagers, as well as his peers who came from other immigrant households.

Jason felt confused, for he did not know which group of friends would meet his parents' approval. He described many fights with his mother and, particularly his father, over this issue. He also argued with his sisters who were beneath him in family status. His mother believed it was her duty to be a perfect mother and protect her children from "bad American influences." She was unaware of her boundary issues and intrusiveness. She would call Jason every hour, wanting to know where he was and whom he was with.

In his work with me, Jason felt free to express his political ideas and sociological stance in regard to the United States and his parents' country of origin, Iraq. He had heard stories about Iraq and Saddam Hussein's cruelty to his people because of being Kurdish minorities Jason knew his parents had immigrated because they were afraid of staying in a war-stricken country, should the regime change hands. They vocalized disdain toward the country's ruler and recalled how they had planned to leave Iraq before living there became impossible.

Jason's family supported the war against Saddam's regime. Initially, Jason had some fear that I would have anti-war sentiments. However, over time, he became confident I would support his ideas. Initially he believed, if he spoke seriously and convincingly with passion, he would be able to influence me and change my mind. This had a familiar ring. I told him I believed he wanted to change my opinion about the war just as he wanted to convince his father of his interest in international relations. In fact, he was quite certain his conviction would persuade me.

Jason made multiple attempts to choose a love object in order to separate himself from his close ties with his mother. In particular, he felt that a relationship with a certain young girl, whom he used in a developmental way, would create the desired separation. The girl, however, met with his parents' disapproval. They insisted that if Jason were ever to go out with her, or think of marrying her, he would face their disapproval. His parents made it clear that a relationship with a girl who did not come from his ethnic background was not an option for him. He knew that his parents would push him toward a Kurdish union in the future. He also realized he needed to examine his ambivalent feelings about his mother and fear of his father's aggression.

Although Jason admired his father, he was afraid of his father's temper. His solution was to spend more time in the company of his mother and avoid talking to his father. This was a familiar theme from his oedipal period, when he showed a desire to be with his mother and resented the presence of his father and later the newborn sister. The re-emergence of the oedipal theme in Jason's adolescent phase was significant. The earlier developmental anxieties of the phallic-oedipal phase once again reappeared in this treatment phase.

The experience of accent

Jason understood the Kurdish language but could not speak it in an articulate way. He was the translator of his mother's emotional and language worlds. He had never objected to his role as translator in his family, even though he often felt burdened by it.

In one of his later sessions, Jason shared his feelings about his parents' accent. He reported that, whenever he invited a friend over to his house, he secretly hoped his mother would be out shopping with her friends. I suggested that because he speaks fluent English when he hears his mother's accent, a discontinuity is created in his mind as if he sensed discordance in the flow of their conversational interaction.

Jason also expressed concern over the way his conversations with his mother may have sounded to his friends. I reminded him that he knew I also have an accent, and earlier he had been curious about the country from where I had emigrated. He replied that when he had asked about my accent in an early session, I made him guess. That same evening, he reported, he had asked his mother where I was from, and she told him. After that, he stopped asking about my accent.

Cultural differences

Jason enumerated multiple areas of cultural gap between his parents' culture and that of the American families he'd come to know. His sensitivity in identifying differences in the outside world extended in a parallel way to his ability to recognize differences between his thoughts and feelings and those of his mother. In the middle phase of his analysis, Jason expressed a wish that his mother would allow him to be different and not expect him to be the kind of son who has views identical to hers.

I pointed out that he was keen about our differences too, especially now that he was moving closer to the end of our work. I added that he knows he has his own sense of agency and separateness, which is different from his mother and me. I have added that he is also worried, that if he becomes too separated from her, he will lose her love and my caring feelings for him as well. At this point, Jason lapsed into silence, thought some more, and then nodded.

As we neared the end of his second half of analysis, Jason, who was a handsome young man, began dyeing his hair even more frequently than before, in order to look Western. His fair skin and altered hair color gave him the illusion of being of "European descent." This change in his appearance, a result of dyeing his hair, took place around the time of the attack on Iraq and again during his termination period. Jason denied experiencing anxiety over the war in Iraq. He reported that it was his father who would sit glued to the television, obsessed about all the details of the war. This was his defense against identification with his parental socio-political and ethnic identity.

The search for a consolidated ethnic identity

Jason struggled to find his own self and the ability to form a more reliable sense of self-identity. In particular, he wished for a more consolidated sense of ethnic identity but was ambivalent about identifying with his mother. In this respect, having to rely on his newly formed sense of American-ness was tenuous. Did he have a Kurdish-Iraqi part within, as did his parents, or was his identity connected to an Anglo-American identity? At home, Jason spoke English to his parents, while his parents answered him in Kurdish. Although he understood most of what they said, he could not speak Kurdish. He felt left out when his parents conversed in their mother tongue.

This linguistic intimacy between his parents excluded Jason from the parental couple and initiated a re-emergence of the oedipal conflict. This old, yet new version of the conflict presented Jason with a new reminder that his parents had their own separate existence; and functioned as a unit in their couple relationship while he felt like an outsider.

Jason's view of his parents' customs, language, dress, and other sociological phenomena permitted him to identify with them, and yet, also made him ambivalent as to how to identify with the new parental mores. His view of his struggles toward identity formation must have caused Jason inner turmoil and threatened identity diffusion, subsequently giving rise to an overwhelming anxiety.

He was dismayed with their relative absence of parental influence and not maintaining more consistently a continuity of their long-held customs and values. His parents defensively adhered to an ethnocentric mode of existence, insisting that Jason would have to comply with their wishes. This was evident regarding their ideas about clothing and appearance. The parents' integration into the new host country encountered impediments of many kinds, which resulted in a sense of powerlessness, loss of status and their own identity diffusion.

Sexual mores

Jason often felt guilty when he had to keep his attraction toward a female classmate secret. He felt even more guilt when he took the girl to a movie theater and then lied to his parents about where he had been. He told me, "If they knew about it, they would have had a heart attack!" We discussed the dilemma he was in and listed the pros and cons of revealing and concealing the news from his parents. Jason responded that once he turned eighteen, his parents would no longer be able to do anything about it. Then, he will be able to do what he wants with his life. Until then, however, he will have to wait. His mother's sexual mores were completely different from those in their American host country. Dating, sexual activity or experimentation with the opposite sex did not belong to her world. It was difficult for me to discuss with his mother what is considered normal adolescent sexuality in Anglo-American culture, she was unwilling to accept it. On the other hand, it was necessary for Jason to keep his thoughts and behavior to himself and for me to keep it confidential.

Vying for control

During Jason's senior year of high school, after his acceptance into several prestigious universities, his parents decided to make plans for him to live at home and attend a nearby community college. They were convinced he would be better off under their supervision and told me they believed that he would avoid getting into drugs and drinking alcohol if he lived at home. Jason was furious with his parents' decision. He felt his mother was controlling him and this was her way of feeling empowered and regaining her lost status. After many sessions with Jason's parents, they agreed to support their son's desire to attend a university a few hours away and live in the dorm. Although my work with Jason was time-limited, but he had the benefit of four-times-weekly psychotherapy for one year, and he made good, observable developmental gains. It is hard to know where he would be, had he not entered treatment. Both Jason and his family were hopeful, open-minded, and motivated.

Conclusion and discussion

Jason's case presents us with several important aspects of the immigrant mother's identity, cultural values and their influence on her son's identity formation as he goes through various stages of development and psychic reorganization.

The influences of the language, self-identity, loss, and mourning, and a sense of not belonging in a new host country are important factors which impact, in a parallel process, respectively the psychic structures of the immigrant mother and her adolescent child's separation-individuation and oedipality. His journey through various phases of his developmental migration, presents a challenge for his necessary, age-appropriate adolescent transformative changes.

The adolescent emigrates from the family and moves into a world of freedom, supposedly functioning autonomously at the end of the latency period. The developmental/psychological migration of an adolescent is important in order to establish an optimal distance from his mother to achieve completion of his individuation. At the same time, the psychic equilibrium of the immigrant mother is affected by the new host country's expectation that she be able to acculturate without delay. If the cultural settings of the host country are hostile or traumatizing, they can adversely affect the psychological equilibrium of the mother.

The integration of maternal ambivalent feelings is particularly crucial, because the immigrant mother struggles to resolve her own ambivalence in order to offer her ego strengths to her adolescent child. She will have to help him further to resolve his developmental conflicts during this phase of adolescence. Her ambivalence might be pervasive, but as seen here, is particularly noticeable by how often she uses the new language and how frequently she reverts to using the mother tongue.

Adolescent progressive and regressive experiences and incorporation of his maternal cultural and ethnic upbringing become more exaggerated. Thus the adolescent has a much more difficult task to reconcile his identification with his immigrant mother. The adolescent's task becomes even more daunting when the mother is struggling to solidify her own sense of multicultural identity, having to overcome her ambivalence. The mother may experience the distancing of her child as more of a threat during the second rapprochement phase of adolescence. The threat to her ego integrity could prevent her from being fully present to help her child's ego strengths and identity integration. Thus, both the mother and child's newly acquired self-representations, as well as their old self-representations of mother and child can become more vulnerable and subject to fragmentation during this process.

A mother and her son's respective developmental lines intersect and influence one another. The mother's projections of her self-representation onto the adolescent can increase the internal conflict of an already troubled sense of newly acquired American identity, as well as her previous, yet present and alive, ethnic identity. Establishing a sexual identity, as part of overall self-identity, can present conflicts, as well.

If the immigrant mother has conflicts around her child's sense of loyalty to the host country and her own dis-identification with American culture or language, then the individuation process and formation of intimacy outside of the family setting can become even more problematic. Furthermore, the establishment of mastery and control over libidinal and aggressive drives by means of restructuring the psychic apparatus (including the ego, superego, and the ego ideal) can present difficulty for the adolescent. Additionally, the final resolution of the Oedipus complex, in both positive and negative aspects, facilitated by temporary regression to an earlier level of conflict in the adolescent phase, would not be without significant psychological repercussions. The final task of genital primacy for adolescents also becomes complicated if the immigrant mother is unable to deal with her ambivalent feelings about new customs, language, sexual mores, and a lack of integration between ethnic identity and newly acquired self-identity.

As Peter Blos suggests (1967, p. 163) in his paper, called "The second individuation process of adolescence," the mandatory part of normal development, in which there is a re-working of the early separation-individuation process of the first three years of life during the adolescent phase, would find a new opportunity to work through a second individuation process, providing the parents have resolved their own conflicts. Parental prohibition prevents the adolescent from forming a peer-object relationship and hinders the individuation process by way of separating from their intra-psychic infantile object ties and dependencies. The process of separating from maternal ties and turning to group affiliation could be problematic.

The regressive and progressive processes accompanied by both depressive affects at the loss of earlier object ties and exhilaration at the development of independent autonomous functioning would be compromised. Adolescents cope with the anxiety and depression created by this process either by withdrawal and inactivity or by motor activity, which may take on frantic proportions in their efforts to escape loneliness and boredom. The ambivalence of early object relations reappears in this phase. The adolescent ego finds the ambivalence intolerable, and it will lead to defensive operations of negativism, oppositionalism, and indifference.

Some adolescents act out their immigration neurosis[7] by rebelling against parental, social, and cultural values. Their rebelliousness has a particular quality of intense forcefulness. It carries with it earlier roots of their unresolved mother-child dyadic conflicts, mis-attunement, and possible attachment disruptions. When the mother's value system within the nuclear family, clashes with her adolescent child's value system, the psychological emancipation of the adolescent becomes strained. Adolescents, in their strong fantasy framework, strive to belong to their new peer group. Parents do not belong to their world, particularly when immigrant parents present a variety of different social and cultural values that are discordant with contemporary culture. Jason's case suggests that both positive and negative aspects of ethnic identification became diluted during his adolescence, while identification with parental mores must have taken place at the same time. In addition, his mother's mourning process at the start of her migration left Jason with unfinished internal work from his first separation-individuation process.

Because of his mother's many migrations and her own mid-life separation-individuation issues, Jason's second, or adolescent separation-individuation process was delayed, too. His oedipal phase was also affected, due to residual unresolved pre-oedipal conflicts and an unfinished first separation-individuation process. His fear of being overpowered and controlled by his mother, his aggressive impulses toward her, and his castration anxiety were the central features of his turmoil. His father, who was not his ally, contributed to his low self-esteem and lack of confidence. His father's loss of

---

7 The author defines "immigration neurosis" as an internal conflict associated with being an immigrant, displaced person or refugee, similar to "traumatic neurosis" or "war neurosis."

status and the absence of cultural support weakened him in Jason's eyes.

Jason's analysis and my parent work with his immigrant mother illustrate an important point: working with an immigrant population requires accommodating the therapeutic framework to cultural differences, assuming the role of a developmental object, and conducting the developmental work to facilitate the individuation process. In working with these types of patients, the analyst can encounter higher degrees of complexity involving a modified analytic technique, special concerns with transference and counter-transference dilemmas, and a more sensitive attunement to cultural and language differences.

CHAPTER 9

On being raised by immigrant mothers: Self and immigrant parenting[8]

The struggle in self-identity formation among immigrant parents and their adolescent children is a complex phenomenon. I approach this topic through my experience with immigrant parents' increasing difficulties in dealing with their adolescent children in the clinical setting. Immigrant families and their children must negotiate between the contrasting American and their own original world by employing different strategies and coping mechanisms to create a transitional condition that would resolve the difficulties between these two worlds. Integration into the new culture requires giving up part of one's sense of individuality. Immigration brings about the loss of what is left behind and a mourning process that is intrapsychically taxing.

On an internal level, the immigrant fluctuates between extremes of distance from his native self-representation and his newly emerging self-representation as a resident of the adopted country. Failure to negotiate the distance between these self-representations results in two problematic outcomes of identity (Teja and Akhtar, 1981): ethnocentric withdrawal and counter-phobic assimilation.

---

8 Originally published as Mann, M. (2004). Immigrant parents and their emigrant adolescents: The tension of inner and outer worlds. *The American Journal of Psychoanalysis*, 64(2): 143–153. https://doi.org/10.1023/B:TAJP.0000027269.37516.16. Reproduced with permission.

As Winnicott (1965) described, "false" and "true" selves alternating phases of closeness and distance from one or the other culture challenge the splitting of the self and the object world. Unlike mature adults, adolescents do not have the inner stability that allows them to control their impulses because they are in the process of integrating their standards of conduct. Adolescents normally look to parents to prevent them from letting their impulses get out of control. They look to their parents in an effort to keep their impulses from overwhelming them.

The immigrant parents struggling with their own sense of identity formation are not emotionally available for their teenage children to offer them the assistance they need to deal with and master their anxiety. Therefore, the strengthening of the ego's efforts to master anxiety in the adolescent phase does not take place.

The adolescent process is characterized by massive upheaval, both physical and psychological, following the relative calm of a latency period. There is increased conflict in many areas, shown by fluctuation between regression and progression, dependency and self-reliance, male versus female, passivity versus activity, and control versus submission. The organizations of the ego, id, and superego lessen, and when this is accompanied by challenges of immigration to a new host country, it could potentially create sets of new outcomes.

The problem is compounded for these parents and their adolescents because simultaneously there are two events. First, the adolescent is involved intra-psychically in the adolescent process of identity formation; second, the parents are involved in the struggle for new self-identity formations in the host country. The process of emancipation from parental control and maturation of self-dependence and creation of an autonomous self would face new challenges. Following are the discussions of three cases that demonstrate the developmental conflicts facing separation-individuation issues and emancipation difficulty from their immigrant parents. The added pressure and strain in such situations is notable.

Case of John, whose mother is Persian and father is East Indian

John, a sixteen-year-old male, was referred to me because of his feelings of depression and lack of focus. The trouble started after his mother was diagnosed with multiple myeloma two years prior. He was not experiencing any trouble with focusing or completing assignments until around the time of his mother's illness.

John's parents emigrated to the United States two years before his birth. His sister was born five years later. John's mother was a very intellectual woman who came from Northern Iran and was a political scientist. His father, a computer engineer, came from Northern India. The couple met in the United States while in graduate school. They returned to their respective countries, decided to become engaged, and married. They married out of love and decided to emigrate to the United States for professional advancement and to form a family. The process of their acculturation was compounded because of the language dissimilarity and cultural and socioeconomic differences.

According to his father, John was the result of a planned pregnancy with normal developmental events. He was described as active, but cooperative, as a toddler and preschooler. When John came to see me, he knew that he was seeing someone from his mother's country. He was intrigued that I knew Farsi, although he knew very few words. He was visibly in a lot of pain and teared up whenever he would make reference to his mother. I suspected that his inattention coinciding with his mother's illness was because of his anticipated maternal loss. He was reluctant to finish his work at school and at home, but he would play computer games for hours. After his mother's death, John stopped coming to therapy for several weeks. When he returned, he could not stop crying and told me how much he missed his mother. Sometimes, he would daydream that his mother would come back, and everything would become as it used to be. He claimed the happiest time he had was when his mother was around, and life was simple. John's schoolwork suffered during this period of the mourning process. John would complain about his social anxiety being with other classmates and the feeling of depression. During this period, he would react by driving his car too fast or taking his father's car without permission. He would have feelings of boredom most of the time and had dreams about his mother's death.

He would not do his work and did not want to think that his mother was gone. Although maternal relatives were at a distance of several hundred miles away from his home, John's father tried to make an effort to visit his aunts and uncle every few months. This was John's only connection with his mother's side of the family. His father would observe holidays and religious days from his own background as well as those of John's mother. Although he looked up to his dad and considered him an honest, disciplined, and successful person, he did not get along with him during that period of mourning. His father avoided most interaction with friends and other family members. John reported that his father was sad and suffering in silence. John reported that the whole family, his sister, his father, and himself, were frustrated and unhappy.

John became attracted to classmates who were from another culture (Asian). He wanted to know how women think. He would briefly get involved and find himself longing for closeness. His greatest fear was that he would never be able to get married and would die alone. Somehow, he would repeatedly end up feeling rejected by his girlfriends. The process of his loss of object and the mourning of these losses would repeat itself.

My work with John continued on a weekly basis, focusing on the mourning process and developing strengths in his ego functioning. John had been exposed at a mid-adolescent age to threats of his mother's death. He was using all of his ego capacity to master her death through his usual defense mechanism. He was overwhelmed and shocked and experienced a state of confusion and disorganization that affected his schoolwork. He attempted to master the situation by repetition and also through erotization of the memories of the traumatic event by getting close to girls and feeling rejected by them. The repetition of feeling rejected might succeed in its task of mastery, or it might be traumatic in itself. John's experience of dating and becoming involved with girls was both.

The trauma and the mourning process gave rise to intense rage and arrested feelings that were forbidden and difficult to handle. John's unconscious conflicts became intensified by the trauma of his mother's death and by having internalized the immigration process of his parents. He viewed this trauma as punishment for some of his conscious or unconscious crimes.

He became inhibited and developed pathogenic defenses against forbidden drives. The trauma produced stimuli that were libidinal in nature and may have increased the intensity of his drive derivatives. Also, his ego was made fragile by trauma, and he was unable to perform autonomous ego functions or to defend successfully against derived derivatives and the anxiety that was evoked.

Although John's present girlfriend seemed to be loving, comforting, and reassuring, he had a great deal of self-doubt and confusion about how he would be able to maintain his relationship with her. John's separation from his mother caused him to be unable to experience his girlfriend as loving and comforting, and he was anxious about keeping the derived satisfaction. The love of a mother, through her talk, touch, words, and comfort, gratifies and provides a means of discharge. The mother also protects the child from environmental over-stimulation with its potentially traumatic effects. Without the presence of his mother, John was possibly traumatized by excessive external stimulation, as well as excessive internal-derived stimulation. He idealized his mother and her image. Because of repeated rejection, he developed a sense of possible mastery over the trauma of his mother's death and earlier resolved acculturations of his parents.

According to Peter Fonagy (2001), the importance of the development of mentalizing self-organization is the exploration of the mental state of the sensitive caregiver who enables the child to find, in his or her mind, an image of the self as motivated by beliefs, feelings, and intentions. There is considerable evidence to support the view that secure attachment enhances the development of inner security, self-worth, and autonomy. When the process of mentalization fails, the integration of self-identity formation and self-organization fails as well.

Case of Kathy, whose mother is Nigerian and father is African American

Kathy was an eighteen-year-old African American girl who came to see me because of depressive symptoms and confusion about her sexual identity. Her father, a successful attorney, practiced law at his own firm. Her mother came to the United States from Nigeria about two decades ago. Her parents met and married here in the United States. Kathy was born two years later, and the couple had another daughter the following year. Kathy's parents divorced when she was younger than two years of age.

In our first session, Kathy related that she was not sure if she was bisexual or homosexual. She then told me that her parents always lived separately, and she had no memory of whether they had ever been together. Her father was mostly absent and would occasionally visit Kathy and her sister. Kathy revealed that her mother had, off and on, experienced depressive symptoms over the years. Kathy tended to be "tomboyish" in preschool and in kindergarten. She described her mother as very loving and protective of her and her sister. Her father only showed interest in her when she began to attend high school. Kathy stated that she enjoyed writing and roller skating. She had difficulty managing her moods, which would swing between hypomanic states and depression. She began using drugs and alcohol, but by the time of referral, she had ceased using either of these substances. When she turned thirteen, her depression worsened, which was when she started using marijuana.

She told me she had a boyfriend, but that she had no desire to engage in sexual relationships with him, although she depended on him and felt she could not leave him. There were times when she felt pressured to have sex with him. She resisted but eventually surrendered to his demands. Kathy was unable to describe to me her feelings about her first sexual experience and reported the experience without affect and a sense that she was supposed to get it over with. Her girlfriends had already started having sex, and she wanted to get it over with, too.

Kathy's unconscious conflict over her belief that she was "male-like" or "masculine" stemmed from her conflicts about being a woman. This conflict, which apparently stemmed from her traumatic and painful interaction with her parents during childhood, possibly led to identification with parents of the opposite sex rather than of the same sex. Even though she appeared very feminine in her manner of dressing and personal care, she had an unconscious identification with her absent father. Kathy's second individuation process had been problematic. The pressure of her impulses during this period of her life resulted in the weakening of her ego and the creation of instability. The absence of family cohesion and a support system prompted Kathy to experiment further with drugs and associate with an unsuitable peer group.

I frequently observed a regression to a close tie with her mother, and its push-and-pull tensions were frequently observed during the course of her treatment. Through these regressive and progressive shifts, Kathy's sexual identity formation was challenged further by the absence of parental figures. Kathy was unable to renounce homoerotic desires to stabilize her sexual identity. Furthermore, her confusion about her ethnic orientation complicated her second separation-individuation process of adolescence. Because of her dis-identification with her maternal ethnic affiliation and social disconnectedness from her mother's heritage, Kathy found herself identifying with her African American father's ethnic background. This would represent a flight from the maternal object tie.

Kathy's treatment continues with my role as a reinforcer of her sense of who she is and differentiating her sexual identity and orientation as well as strengthening her ego function to contain her impulses. In her familial cultural setting, there were conflicts over Kathy's mother assimilation into the middle-class African American lifestyle. Her mother was not welcomed and was treated miserably to the degree that it led to marital discord and subsequent divorce. The early adverse marital conflict continued to affect Kathy's psychic stability in her first and second separation-individuation processes. The confusion about sexual identity and role started early on, which led to an unstable sense of self (Freud, 1933b).

Case of Robert, whose parents are Iraqi

Robert, an eighteen-year-old adolescent male, came to see me because of depression. In our first session, he said, "I feel I am smothered by my parents. When I am around them, I feel down, short-tempered, miserable, and terrible. My whole life should be focused on school only." Robert comes from an Assyrian-Iraqi background. Both parents are from Northern Iraq and have lived in the United States for two decades. His parents are professionals; they left Iraq in their early twenties. Robert has two younger siblings, both girls, aged fifteen and fourteen years. Robert's parents lived in Texas for the first few years of his life, and then they moved to San Jose, California.

Robert went to an all-private boys' school in his middle and high-school years. He failed to do well in his freshman year in college, which he related to the arrangements his parents had made for him to live at home, even though he was accepted at several other universities in the United States and outside the country. Robert was angry with his parents for not permitting him to leave home and enroll in an out-of-state university. They insisted that he live at home and attend a nearby state university. Robert told me that his father finally accepted that he was interested in political science and did not want to become an engineer like him. Although Robert had been a very good student, he failed some courses in his freshman year. He rebelled against his parents' authority and felt he would show them his anger by neglecting his grades. However, he continued to be active in basketball, and his family supported his athletic abilities by taking him on a trip so he could play with an Assyrian basketball team.

Robert's therapy has had many interwoven themes, but my focus has been on his cultural identity and adolescent development process. His parents have been ethnocentric and devalue American culture as being too independent and "wild." They would attribute much of Robert's behavior to the American way and would criticize him. His desire to connect with his peer group, who belonged to other cultural backgrounds, would provoke parental disapproval.

Robert described many fights with his mother and, in particular, his father. He also had arguments with his two younger sisters. His mother was overprotective and intrusive. She would call him every couple of hours wanting to know where he was and who he was with. Robert was able to express his political ideas and sociological stance regarding the United States and his parents' home country, Iraq. He heard about Iraq and Saddam Hussein's cruelty. The family was in support of the war against Saddam's regime. Robert was afraid that I would have anti-war sentiments, but he was sure that I would support his ideas. In fact, he was certain that I would also be in his camp. Unconsciously, he attempted to use me as a maternal object to separate himself from close ties with his mother. He also entered into a relationship with a young woman, who was used in a developmental way, which he believed would separate him from his mother. This relationship was countered with parental disapproval. They feared that if he ever were to marry, he would marry a non-Assyrian girl.

He knew that his parents would be pushing him toward an Assyrian union. He realized that he needed to examine his ambivalent feelings about his mother and his fear of his father's aggression. Although Robert admires his father, he is afraid of his temper.

Robert is a handsome young man with fair skin, yet he has frequently dyed his hair to look more Western. His hair color gave him the illusion that he was of "European descent." This change in his appearance, dyeing his hair, was done around the time of the attack on Iraq, although he denied any anxiety over the war in Iraq. He observed that his father was glued to the television and knew all the details of the war events.

Robert seems to struggle to find himself and form a solid sense of who he is and also a consolidated sense of his ethnic identity. He speaks English to his parents; his parents speak in their Assyrian dialect. Although he understands most of what they say, he cannot speak the language. His view of his parental customs, language, dress, and other sociological phenomena permit him to identify and yet at the same time be ambivalent about which to identify with, the new or the parental mores. His parents were dismayed about their lack of influence on him and his reluctance to continue with their customs and values. Their integration into the new host country encountered impediments and a sense of powerlessness. The parents adhered defensively to an ethnocentric mode of existence, insisting that John would have to comply.

Discussion

The adolescent emigrates from the family and immigrates into a supposedly autonomous world. The process starts at the end of the latency period (A. Freud, 1958). Psychological immigration for adolescents is important to distance them from their family. At the same time, the psychic equilibrium of the immigrant parent of the adolescent is affected by the new host country's environmental factors. If the cultural settings of the host country are hostile or they are not open to the new culture (i.e., Robert's parents), they can adversely affect the psychological equilibrium of the parents. The integration of ambivalent feelings is particularly crucial because immigrant parents must themselves struggle to resolve their own ambivalence to offer their ego strengths to their adolescent children, helping resolve their conflicts. Also, adolescents' progressive and regressive experiences of themselves and the incorporation of their parental cultural and ethnic upbringing become more exaggerated. The adolescents of immigrant parents have a much more difficult task of reconciling their identification with their parents.

The adolescent tasks become even more complex when their parents are struggling to form their own sense of bicultural identity and overcome their ambivalence (Akhtar, 1994, 1999; Mehta, 1998). They will see the distancing of their youngsters as more of a threat during the second rapprochement phase of adolescence. The threat to the parents' ego integrity would not permit them to be emotionally available to help their adolescent with his or her ego strengths and integration of self-identity as well as their own. Therefore, integration of their own core and acquired self-representations suffers further during this process.

The developmental line of the adolescent and the developmental course of their parents intersect and influence one another. The parental projections of their own self-representation to the adolescent would increase the internal conflict of the already troubled sense of core American and acquired ethnic identity self-representation. The establishment of a sense of self-identity and sexual identity would become a challenge to these groups of adolescents. If the immigrant parents have conflict around their children's sense of loyalty to their host country and their identification with American culture, the process of separation-individuation and formations of intimacy outside the family setting would be even more problematic (Mahler, Pine & Bergman 1963).

Furthermore, the establishment of mastery and control over drives, both libidinal and aggressive, by restructuring the psychic apparatus (including the ego, superego, and the ego ideal) would be a challenge for this group. In addition, the final resolution of the Oedipus complex, in both positive and negative aspects and facilitated by temporary regression to an earlier level of conflict in the adolescent phase, would also be a struggle for these young people because the final task of genital primacy for adolescents becomes complicated if the immigrant parents are unable to create their own sense of core identity with their acquired self-identity.

As Blos indicated (1962, 1967), the mandatory part of normal development, in which there is a re-working of the early separation-individuation process of the first three years of life during the adolescent phase, would find an opportunity to work through a second individuation process, providing the parents are endowed with their own resolved conflicts. Parental prohibition prevents the adolescent from forming a peer–object relationship and hinders the individuation process by way of separating from their intra-psychic infantile object ties and dependencies. The process of separating from family ties and turning to group affiliation would pose problems. The regressive and progressive processes accompanied by both depressive affects at the loss of earlier object ties and exhilaration at the development of independent autonomous functioning would be compromised. Adolescents cope with the anxiety and depression created by this process either by withdrawal and inactivity or by motor activity, which may take on frantic proportions in their efforts to escape loneliness and boredom. The ambivalence of early object relations again reappears in this phase. The adolescent ego finds the ambivalence intolerable, and it will lead to the defensive operations of negativism, oppositionalism, and indifference (Giovacchini, 1973).

In addition, we see a re-working of oedipal conflicts among adolescents. The oedipal situation begins with the child's recognition of the parents' relationship. The failure to internalize a recognizable oedipal triangle results in a failure to integrate observation and experience. The complex unfolds further in the development of the child's rivalry with one parent for absolute possession of the other. Through mourning for this lost exclusive relationship, it can be realized that the oedipal triangle does not translate into the death of a relationship. Parents who have an unresolved oedipal complex contribute to the problem of their adolescents' identity formation and further complicate the struggle in mourning for their exclusive relationship. Consequently, we see the immigration process becoming much more complicated.

Young people use different styles in their adolescent immigration. Some act out their emigration neurosis toward their parents. They rebel against parental social and cultural values. When there is a clash between the value systems of two parents in a nuclear family, it puts a strain on the psychological emancipation of adolescents. Because most young people immigrate into the next developmental phase, they move first to the actual contemporaries of their own peer group. Through their introject, they also want to move to the next developmental phase in terms of anticipation of its particular function.

Adolescents in their strong fantasy framework strive to belong to their new peer group. Parents do not belong to their world, particularly if the immigrant parents present a variety of different social and cultural values discordant to the contemporary culture. The cases of John, Kathy, and Robert suggest that both positive and negative aspects of ethnic identification get diluted during adolescence when identification with parental mores occurs. Adolescents of immigrant families have much more complicated tasks during this phase of their lives to establish a future sense of self-identity. A well-consolidated sense of self-identity is more complicated for these types of multiethnic immigrant families. The adolescent would have to rely on parental ego function and their parents' coherent sense of identity to weather this stage of turbulent times.

References

Ackman, P. (2012). Helping the helpers: Consultation to childcare staff using psychoanalytically informed developmental concepts. *Psychoanalytic Inquiry, 32*: 186–204.

Akhtar, S. (1994). A third individuation: Immigration, identity, and the psychoanalytic process. *Journal of the American Psychoanalytic Association, 43*: 1051–1084.

——— (1999). *Immigration and Identity: Turmoil, Treatment, and Transformation*. Northvale, NJ: Jason Aronson.

——— (2004). Special issue: Immigration and the lifecycle. *American Journal of Psychoanalysis, 64*.

——— (2011). *Immigration and Acculturation: Mourning, Adaptation, and the Next Generation*. Lanham, MD: Jason Aronson.

Allison, G. H. (1997). Motherhood, motherliness, and psychogenic infertility. *Psychoanalytic Quarterly, 66*: 1–17.

Amado, P.S.M. Woodley, C. Cristiano, M.L.S. & O'Neill, P.M. (2022). Recent Advances of DprE1 Inhibitors against Mycobacterium Tuberculosis: Computational Analysis of Physicochemical and ADMET Properties. *ACS Omega* 7:40659–40681.

Amati-Mahler, J. (1995). The exiled language. *Canadian Journal of Psychoanalysis, 3*: 87–104.

American Psychological Association (2012) *Crossroads: The psychology of immigration in the new century*, APA Presidential Task Force on Immigration. http://www.apa.org/topics/immigration/report.asp

Amsterdam, B. (1972). Mirror self-image reactions before age two. *Developmental Psychobiology, 5*(4): 297–305.

Benedek, T. (1952). *Psychosocial Functions in Women*. New York: Ronald Press.

Bibring, G., Dwyer, T. F., Huntington, D. S., & Valenstein, A. F. (1961). A study of psychological process in pregnancy and of the earliest mother and child relationship. *Psychoanalytic Study of the Child*, 16: 9–72.

Blos, P. (1962). *On Adolescence*. New York: Free Press.

______ (1967). The second individuation process of adolescence. *Psychoanalytic Study of the Child*, 22: 162–186.

Bowlby, J. (1984) Violence in the Family as a Disorder of the Attachment and Caregiving Systems. *American Journal of Psychoanalysis* 44:9–27.

Brazelton, T.B., & Als, H. (1979). Four early stages in the development of mother-infant interaction. *Psychoanalytic Study of the Child*, 34: 349–369.

Broucek, F.J. (1982). Shame and its relationship to early narcissistic developments. *International Journal of Psychoanalysis*, 63: 369–378.

Brown, D, & De Cao, E, (2020). Child Maltreatment, Unemployment, and Safety Nets, *SSRN*. http://dx.doi.org/10.2139/ssrn.3543987

——— (1991). *Shame and the Self*. New York: Guilford.

Campbell, D. (2012) NHS told to improve care for women in early pregnancy. *The Guardian*, UK, Wednesday, December 12, 2012.

Confortini, C.C., & Ruane, A.E. (2014). Sara Ruddick's Maternal Thinking as weaving epistemology for justpeace. *Journal of International Political Theory* 10(1): 70–93. https://doi.org/10.1177/1755088213507187

Deutsch, H. (1945). *The Psychology of Women (II)*. New York: Grune and Stratton.

Diedrich, K., Fauser B.C., Devroey, P,, Diedrich C. (2007), In Vitro Fertilization. *New England Journal of Medicine* 56(1): 50–61. doi:10.1056/NEJMcp065743

Ehrensaft, D. (2008a). When baby makes three or four or more. *Psychanalytic Study of the Child* 63: 3–23.

Ehrensaft, D. (2008b). Mommies, Daddies, Donors, Surrogates: Answering Tough Questions and Building Strong Families.

Emde, R.N. (1983). The pre-representational self and its affective core. *Psychoanalytic Study of the Child 38*: 165–192.

Farrokhzad, F. (2004). The abandoned house. *Collected Poems*. M. Mann (Trans.). Tehran, Iran: Shadan Publishing Company, in Farsi.

Ferguson, T.J., Stegge, H., & Damhuis, I. (1991). Children's understanding of guilt and shame. *Child Development 62*(4): 827–839.

Field, T.M., Woodson, R., Greenberg, R., & Cohen, D. (1982). Discrimination and imitation of facial expressions by neonates. *Science 218*(4568): 179–181.

Fonagy, P. (2001). *Attachment Theory and Psychoanalysis*. New York: Other Press.

———Gergely, G., Jurist, E. L., & Target, M. (2002). *Affect Regulation, Mentalization, and the Development of the Self*. Other Press.

———Target, M., Gergely, G., Allen, J. G. & Bateman, A. W. (2003). The Developmental Roots of Borderline Personality Disorder in Early Attachment Relationships: A Theory and Some Evidence. *Psychoanalytic Inquiry* 23:412–459.

Freud, A. (1936). *The Ego and the Mechanisms of Defense. In The Writings of Anna Freud* (Vol. 2, pp. 3-191). New York, NY: International Universities Press. (1958). Adolescence. *Psychoanalytic Study of the Child 13*: 1–3.

Freud, S. (1914). Remembering, repeating and working-through: Further recommendations on the technique of psycho-analysis II. *S.E. 12*: 145–157. London: Hogarth.

—— (1920). Beyond the Pleasure Principle. *S.E., 18*: 7–64.

—— (1923). The ego and the id. *S.E., 19*: 12–66.

—— (1926). Inhibitions, Symptoms and Anxiety. *S. E., 20*: 75–176.

—— (1930) Civilization and its Discontents. *S.E., 21*: 57–46.

—— (1933a) Why War?. The Standard Edition of the Complete Psychological Works of Sigmund Freud 22:1953–216

—— (1933b) Lecture XXXIII Femininity. In New Introductory Lectures On Psycho-Analysis. *S.E.* 22:1–182.

—— (1938). An outline of psychoanalysis. *S.E., 23*: 139–208.

Giovacchini, P.L. (1973). Character development and the adolescent process. In: S. C. Feinstein & P. L. Giovacchini (Eds.), *Adolescent psychiatry* (Vol. 2, pp. 402–414). New York: Basic Books.

Goleman, D. (1989, January 24). Sad legacy of abuse: The search for remedies. *New York Times*.

Greenacre, P. (1941) The Predisposition to Anxiety. *Psychoanalytic Quarterly* 10:66–94

Inderbitzin, L.B., & Levy, S. (1998). Repetition compulsion revisited: Implication for technique. *Psychoanalytic Quarterly, 67*: 32–53.

International Organization for Migration (IOM). (2006). *Female Migration: Bridging the Gaps Throughout the Life Cycle*. New York: IOM.

James, W, (1890). *The Principles of Psychology*, Volume 1 Scotts Valley, CA: CreateSpace Independent Publishing Platform, 2017.

Katan, A. (1961) Some Thoughts about the Role of Verbalization in Early Childhood. *Psychoanalytic Study of the Child 16*: 184–188.

Kaufman, G. (1985). *Shame: The Power of Caring*. Rochester, VT: Shenkman Books.

Kubie, L.S. (1939). A critical analysis of the concept of a repetition compulsion. *International Journal of Psychoanalysis 20*: 390–402.

Lansky, M.R. & Morrison, P.M. (1997). *The Widening Scope of Shame.* London and New York: Routledge.

Lester, E.P., & Notman, M. (1986). Pregnancy, developmental crisis and object relations: psychoanalytic considerations. *International Journal of Psychoanalysis 62*: 357–366.

Lew, M. (2002). *Victims No Longer: The Classic Guide for Men Recovering from Sexual Child Abuse.* New York: Harper Perennial.

Lewis, M. (1992). Will the real self or selves please stand up? *Psychological Inquiry 3*(2): 123–124.

Lichtenberg, J. (1988). Infant research and self-psychology. *Progress in Self Psychology 3*: 59–64.

Loewald, H.W. (1979) The Waning of the Oedipus Complex. *Journal of the American Psychoanalytic Association 27*: 751–775

Ludden, J. (2011). A new openness for donor kids about their biology. *NPR.* https://www.npr.org/2011/09/17/140476716/a-new-openness-for-donor-kids-about-their-biology (last accessed July 27, 2022).

Mahler, M., Pine, F., & Bergman, A. (1963). *The Psychological Birth of the Human Infant.* New York: Basic Books.

Mann, M. (2004). Immigrant parents and their emigrant adolescents. *American Journal of Psychoanalysis 64*: 143–153.

———— (2014). *Psychoanalytic Aspects of Assisted Reproductive Technology.* London: Karnac.

Marks, A. K., Ejesi, K., & Coll, C. G. (2014). Understanding the U.S. Immigrant Paradox in Childhood and Adolescence. *Child Development Perspectives*, 8(2), 59–64.

Mehta, P. (1998). The emergence, conflicts, and integration of the bi-cultural self: Psychoanalysis of an adolescent daughter of south-

Asian immigrant parents. In: S. Akhtar & S. Kramer (Eds.), *The Colors of Childhood: separation-individuation Across Cultural, Racial, and Ethnic Differences* (pp. 129–168). Northvale, NJ: Jason Aronson.

Moore, B., & Fine, B. (1990). *Psychoanalytic Terms and Concepts*. New Haven: Yale University Press.

Morrison, A.P. (1994). The breadth and boundaries of a self-psychological immersion in shame. *Psychoanalytic Dialogues 4*: 19–35.

Nachtigall, R., & Mehren, E. (1991). *Overcoming Infertility: A Practical Strategy for Navigating the Emotional, Medical and Financial Minefields of Trying to Have a Baby*. New York: Doubleday.

Notman, M., & Lester, E.P. (1988). Pregnancy: Theoretical considerations. *Psychoanal. Inq. 8*: 139–160.

Parens, H. (1977). *The Internal Mother: Conceptual and Technical Aspects of Object Constancy*. Jason Aronson.

———— (2015). The changing morphology of parenthood: Its implications for separation-individuation theory. In: S. Akhtar (Ed.), *The New Motherhoods: Patterns of Early Child Care in Contemporary Culture* (pp. XX–XX). Lanham: Rowman & Littlefield.

Perez-Foster, R. (2001). When immigration is trauma: Guidelines for the individual and family clinician. *American Journal of Orthopsychiatry 71*(2): 153–170.

Perry, B.D., Pollard, R.A., Blakley, T.L., Baker, W.L. and Vigilante, D. (1995). Childhood trauma, the neurobiology of adaptation, and "use-dependent" development of the brain: How "states" become "traits". *Infant Ment. Health J., 16*: 271–291.

Pianta, R., Egeland, B., & Erickson, M.F. (1989). The antecedents of maltreatment: Results of the Mother–Child Interaction Research Project. In: D. Cicchetti & V. Carlson (Eds.), *Child Maltreatment:*

REFERENCES

Theory and Research on the Causes and Consequences of Child Abuse and Neglect (pp. 203–253). Cambridge: Cambridge University Press.

Pine, F., Mann, M., & Smith, J.M. (2003). *A Potent Spell: Mother Love and the Power of Fear*. Boston: Houghton Mifflin.

Pines, D. (1982). Relevance of early development to pregnancy and abortion. *International Journal of Psychoanalysis 61*: 311–318.

Schore, A. (1994). The dialogical self and the emergence of consciousness. In: A. Schore (Ed.), *Affect Regulation and the Origin of the Self: The Neurobiology of Emotional Development* (pp. 490–498). Hillsdale, NJ; England: Lawrence Erlbaum Associates, Inc.

Searles, H.F. (1986). *My Work with Borderline Patients*. Northvale, NJ: Jason Aronson.

———— (2005). The psychic landscape of mothers. In: S. F. Brown (Ed.), *What Do Women Want? Developmental Perspectives, Clinical Challenges* (pp. 3–18). New York: Routledge.

Smith, J.M. (2003). *A Potent Spell: Mother Love and the Power of Fear*. New York: Houghton Mifflin.

Teja, J.S., & Akhtar, S. (1981). The psychosocial problems of FMG's with special reference to those in psychiatry. In: R. S. Cohen (Ed.), *Foreign Medical Graduates in Psychiatry: Issues and Problems* (pp. 321–338). New York: Human Sciences Press.

Tomkins, S. (1963). *Affect, Imagery, Consciousness, Vol. II, the Negative Affects*. New York: Springer.

Tsai, T., Chen, I., & Huang, S. (2011). Motherhood journey through the eyes of immigrant women. *Women's Studies International Forum 34*(2): 91–100.

Tummala-Narra, P. (2004). Mothering in a foreign land. *The American Journal of Psychoanalysis 64*(2): 167–181.

——— (2009) Contemporary Impingements on Mothering. *American Journal of Psychoanalysis* 69:4–21.

——— (2013). Women immigrants: Developmental shifts in the new culture. In: L. Comas-Diaz & B. Greene (Eds.), *Psychological Health of Women of Color: Intersections, Challenges, and Opportunities* (pp. 257–274). Westport, CT: Praeger.

Twemlow, S. W., Fonagy, P., & Sacco, F. C. (2005). A developmental approach to mentalizing communities: II. The Peaceful Schools experiment. *Bulletin of the Menninger Clinic, 69*(4): 282–304. https://doi.org/10.1521/bumc.2005.69.4.282

UNICEF (2006). The State of the World's Children 2006: Excluded and Invisible. New York: UNICEF.

Department of Health and Human Services. (2018). Child Maltreatment 2018. Administration for Children and Families.

Van Voorhis, B.J. (2007). In-vitro fertilization. *New England Journal of Medicine 356*: 379–386.

Winnicott, D.W. (1965). *The Family and Individual Development.* London: Tavistock.

——— (1965). *The Family and Individual Development.* London: Tavistock.

——— (1969) The Use of an Object. *International Journal of Psychoanalysis 50*:711–716.

——— (1971). *Playing and Reality.* New York: Routledge.

Young, L. (1954). *Out of Wedlock.* New York: McGraw-Hill.

Zalusky, S. (1999). Infertility in the age of technology. *Journal of the American Psychoanalytic Association 48*: 1541–1562.

www.ingramcontent.com/pod-product-compliance
Lightning Source LLC
Chambersburg PA
CBHW071617030726
47598CB00001B/309